BEYOND BEAUTY

BEYOND BEAUTY JANE PRATT
JANE PRATT BEYOND BEAUTY
BEYOND BEAUTY JANE PRATT
JANE PRATT BEYOND BEAUTY
BEYOND BEAUTY JANE PRATT
JANE PRATT BEYOND BEAUTY
BEYOND BEAUTY JANE PRATT

Edited by Antoinette White and Alexandra Arrowsmith

Designed by Jennifer Wagner

Booth-Clibborn Editions
London
1997

A Callaway Book

To my beautiful mom

Published in the U.K., Ireland, Australia and New Zealand by

Booth-Clibborn Editions

12 Percy Street

London W1P 9FB

Web Site: http://www.booth-clibborn-editions.co.uk

E-Mail: info@internos.co.uk

ISBN: 1-86154-091-4

All photographs which are attributed to named photographers, except as noted herein, are copyrighted by the photographers.

Christy Bush was commissioned to take many of the contemporary photographs reproduced in this book. These are indicated by the initials "CB."

Photograph of Natalie Portman on the cover by Albert Watson. Makeup by Leslie Lopez. Hair by Didier Malige.

Frontispiece: Kirsten Dunst by Christy Bush.

Printed in China

Why I Did This Book

15 was the year beauty consumed me. Until then, I'd always assumed I was pretty enough. Meaning not enough to be a model or Miss America (which my sister Amy and I watched religiously every year). But more important, not ever feeling it was important – especially if I wasn't considering either of those occupations. My mom had grown up never feeling pretty enough herself, so she made sure to tell me regularly that I was. I also remember my mom commenting often on the prettiness of girls who would not have been considered pretty by beauty pageant or magazine standards. When I was 12, a photographer friend of hers took me to the park and took tons of black-and-white photos of me looking very comfortable in my overalls and egghead hair style.

Meanwhile, the school I went to from the fifth grade on, Carolina Friends School, was the coolest. Their whole philosophy was to emphasize the community over the individual. It was all about no grades, open classrooms, and valuing your kite-making skills way more than how silky your hair looked. None of us wore any makeup or did anything time-consuming to make our faces or our bodies any different than they were naturally. We ran cross-country because we loved it, loved running farther and farther – up to 15 miles one day, and loved the cute young cross-country coach, *not* because we wanted to burn calories or tighten our quads.

So it wasn't until I left home to go to boarding school at 15 that I learned about the value, the currency, of beauty. I remember being homesick one day during my first semester and crying to my dormmate, who tried to console me by saying, "But you're one of the pretty girls in school!" And I thought, "Yeah, I am, so are you, so are all of us, and so what?" I couldn't understand how that was supposed to make me feel better. Now I see how rare it was that I got to be 15 before learning that beauty was supposed to take care of you. I'd really thought that it was just on Miss America that girls were pitted against each other based on how strictly they fit into one long-blond-haired, light-skinned, small-nosed, size-four-swimsuited, long-toned-legged, big-breasted mold. And where the winners got everything handed to them – well, money and travel and a tiara, anyway – and got to be the only people I'd ever seen so happy that they smiled and cried at the same time, while waving "thank you, thank you" over and over again. Meanwhile back in my dormroom, I thanked my friend for her compliment and smiled, then went and cried even harder.

That's the year I started to value it. I cut my hair so it was all layered, and learned to use a curling iron to make it flip back sort of Farrah-style around my face. I wore so much makeup that it took me two hours to get ready in the morning – and if I overslept, I'd easily skip class before I'd go out with less than the usual amount. That included undereye coverup stick, then dark foundation in the hollows of my cheeks and down the sides of my nose (for a lovely sculpting effect), multiple shades of blush, a sparkly pink highlighter on my cheekbones. Electric blue (not a color found in nature) eyeliner on the inside of my lower lid and metallic sky blue underneath the lower lashes and a navy blue pencil over the top lashes. Lipliner, lipstick, then Strawberry Kissing Slicks, the kind with the wand. Plus so much mascara that I used to separate my eyelashes with a nail. I also used the money I made cashiering at the mall over the summer to buy a bunch of sweaters in hot pink and turquoise, which I decided were my colors, and a pair of five-inch ankle-strap pointy-toed fake-snakeskin heels.

That was also the year I decided to start *Sassy*. In the middle of all this revamping and flaw-fixing, I realized there might be another way. I had read *Seventeen* magazine pretty regularly since I was about 12 and, alongside the hair and makeup tips, I'd gotten used to seeing these girls that I would never in a million years resemble, no matter how many hours I spent applying products to my face. They were all tall, skinny, mostly blond and blue-eyed, with little noses and little hips and thighs, and they always looked happy and had boys hovering around them constantly. What if there was a magazine that made me (and other girls who didn't relate to those models) feel good about those things that made us different? A magazine that said that big hips and big noses and freckles and all shades of skin and all heights and all weights were beautiful. And that beauty comes much more from what's going on inside your head anyway.

About ten years later, *Sassy* got launched. And since that first realization when I was 15, not a lot had changed in the general beauty standards for young women. The cult of sameness has even grown. I remember in high school all the students making a big deal out of one girl who came back from summer vacation with a newly small upturned nose. Since then, plastic surgery procedures have increased more dramatically among teenagers than any other age group. And while it used to be almost exclusively nose jobs, girls undergo procedures that didn't even exist back then, like liposuction, lip injections, and something called "the waif face," where they scoop the fat pads out of girls' cheeks. Now breast implants are regularly performed on teenagers, whereas women used to at least wait to see their matured bodies first.

At the same time, the cult of small-ness has also led increasing numbers of young women to anorexia and bulimia. And I'll fight with anyone who says that media images of women have no part in this. I mean, boys and girls grow up seeing again and again images of the bodies to strive for. Then, as boys reach adolescence, their bodies naturally grow closer to the male ideal. But when girls hit puberty, their hormones take them further and further away from the photo of the Kate Moss-type figure they have hanging on their bedroom walls. And that's the time in girls' lives when eating disorders most commonly begin.

That's where this book comes in. I thought long and hard about even doing it. Because if there's one thing we don't need, it's more emphasis placed on beauty for young women. But what we do need now, even more than when I was a teenag-er, is to expand the definition of what beauty for young women is. So when I sat down with my pals at Callaway, Sandy and Antoinette, to compile our list of subjects for this book, I knew I wanted a whole range, from the American beauty-pageant ideal I grew up with to young women from vastly different cultures. From girls whose beauty makes them tons of money modeling; to girls whose jobs – like actresses or ballerinas – have traditionally required conforming to a narrow ideal; to girls who say they have no need or desire to think about their looks much at all. Some of the girls featured in here were girls I already knew, like my good buddy Summer Phoenix. I've always thought if I could be like anyone when I grow up, have as much confidence and style and energy, that'd be Summer. I'd also met Christina Ricci one night when our mutual friend Kevin decided on the spur of the moment that we should all three walk across the Brooklyn Bridge for pizza at around midnight. I'd always loved Christina's act-ing, but while we walked and walked and talked, I found she also had such smart things to say on beauty, having grown up in an industry that emphasizes it beyond belief and somehow managing to main-tain her own strong sense of what beauty is. Then other girls found me. Like Hilary

Small. Hilary and I met in Las Vegas. I was there with my friend Drew Barrymore (sounds like name-dropping, I know, but it's an integral part of the story, so shut up). And Drew spotted this truly cool androgynous-looking girl playing slot machines. We immediately worshipped her. She was wearing a white muscle-T with her hair sticking up like a rooster and the greatest easy confidence. Actually, she was kind of like Drew's *doppelgänger*. Her style at the time reminded me so

Jane at 15

much of Drew's that I wondered if she'd intentionally modeled herself after her. It wasn't until we'd all been hanging out for a couple of hours and Hilary asked me what we both did, that I realized Hilary's style was all her own. Although Hilary is still saying she doesn't know why she's in this book, to me she's exactly what this book is about – girls defining beauty for themselves.

Some of the girls profiled here I'd never met before but are girls who epitomize certain beauty standards – maybe you've looked at them in movies or in advertisements and thought you wished you could look like them. Girls like Filippa and Christie Woods. One thing that struck me was the girls who had gone through the same sort of shift I went through at 15 – from feeling beautiful naturally without ever giving it much thought, to a more obsessive and narrow take on how they should look. In this case, the change was most apparent

in the girls who'd recently moved to the United States. Not surprising, since our beauty standards are way more rigid than most other cultures, and since there's a lot more emphasis on the importance of beauty here. As sad as it is to see girls being influenced in this prescriptive, prohibitive direction, I'm hoping that here the reverse will be true – that you girls reading this book can be influenced by the incredible variety of outlooks, styles, and cultural norms presented here towards a less regimented, more encompassing attitude about your own looks.

The idea with all of these girls is not to hold yourselves up to them for comparison, to try to emulate their rou-tines and rituals, or to stand in front of the mirror trying to pose your lips like theirs. It's to see how many types of beautiful there are, to see that your nose and lips and eyes and legs are just as cool as any of theirs. And to see the views of girls who look at beauty very differently – whether because they are from another culture, because they are legally blind like Sharon, or because they have seen the damage that a narrow ideal can bring and have chosen to reject it. As I have. It's in light of that kind of pressure that I just love and respect so much the young women who are challenging our notion of what beauty is, often as living examples.

One of my biggest goals, since that terrible year when I worried more about my eyebrows than my parents' divorce, has been to expand the definition of what's beautiful for young women. To show that beautiful is confidence, beautiful is smart, beautiful is dedication, beautiful is quirky, fat, thin, tall, short, and that beautiful is unusual rather than samesamesame. And I hope to expand the definition starting with some of the gorgeously beautiful girls in this book.

Alison Firestone

Equestrienne
19 years old
Born and lives in Virginia, U.S.A.

BY JAMES LESLIE PARKER

Alison Firestone has broken her nose four times – each break came as she fell from a horse while competing in professional show jumping. She can breathe through her nose, but she's lost her sense of smell, which leads her to believe she probably has a deviated septum. Alison hasn't fixed it yet because she doesn't have the time; she devotes most every waking minute to caring for her horses.

If pressed, Alison will admit her least favorite feature is her hands, which have worked long and hard for her the past 19 years. "It's because I'm working in the barn all the time, and I always forget to ride with gloves, so I have a bunch of calluses on my fingers," she says.

Once she had to get five stitches in her eyelid when a horse threw her and she hit the ground hard. When she's riding, she often bites her lip in concentration – but that's nothing compared to the equestriennes she's known who've had their collarbones broken or been trampled underfoot. In other words, Alison does not give much thought to the dangers of her sport – she enjoys it too much.

Charlie was her first pony. Her parents, who own and breed racehorses, bought him for Alison when she was so little that she can't remember not having him. Alison grew up on a farm in Upperville, Virginia, "so I was always, always in the barn," she says. When she was younger, though, she suffered from horrible allergies and asthma. "I couldn't be in the barn as much as I wanted to be," she says. "But my dad has asthma too, and he taught me how to deal with it. I've kind of grown out of it now, thank God. But the other day," she adds, "I was cleaning, putting new straw in a stall, and I was thinking, Gosh, I would usually be on the ground wheezing to death. But it wasn't bothering me at all." She says she sometimes wonders if her determination to be around horses helped her overcome the asthma – which would normally be provoked by things like hay and horse hair and manure.

Alison started taking riding lessons when she was about nine, and entered her first show when she was ten. She says she did have some trouble at first: In addition to learning how to jump several obstacles in a row, Alison had to master the proper position on a horse. "It takes many lessons to learn how to sit," she says. "You're sitting up very straight yet you're relaxed and move with the motion of the horse. You don't get to be a grand prix rider by just growing into horses. You have to master your body position on a horse so you can ride effectively." Alison won her first show within the year and hasn't taken a break from competing since then. She's earned national championships as she's moved up the ranks from ponies to riding horses at the grand prix level, where the fences are more than five feet tall. In 1996 alone she won more than $70,000 in competitions, and she now ranks 38th in the world.

I don't really mark down times in my head "when I felt the most/least beautiful." My sport is judged on if you get it done or not – very cut-and-dried. It is not how one does it or what one looks like while one is doing it.

When she was still in high school, Alison would get up at 5:00 or 6:00 in the morning just to ride. In her senior year, she'd leave campus during her free periods to go home and ride one more horse. She'd take blocks of days off to fly to Pennsylvania or Washington, D.C., to compete on the show circuit, then catch up on schoolwork on the flight home. "I definitely sacrificed making friends in high school," she says now, "but I don't really regret it at all. Other kids were a lot different than I was, and they didn't understand why I was gone all the time. But I did have friends at the shows, and I probably saw them more often than my friends from school."

Alison's pals on the show circuit include her horses, which become pets to her. "I think horses are a lot like people," she says, "because each one has a unique personality.  Horses are easier to deal with sometimes because they're more agreeable – they want to please you. I can be completely entertained taking a horse and just turning him out in the fields, just watching him play in the field by himself. I enjoy understanding horses, learning how they behave, because without the horses you're nowhere – you're standing on the ground. Your horse is your partner. You can't consider yourself the bigger percentage because it's a 50/50 partnership."

Even her sartorial style is defined by horses; since she rides every chance she can get, she's in her riding gear 99% of the time. Her outfit, part function and part

Who has taught me about beauty: My horses. Trying to emulate their gracefulness is a lesson in itself.

tradition, includes tall, black leather boots, beige or white breeches, a light-colored cotton shirt, and a riding jacket. The outfit she chooses each day reflects the importance of the classes she contests. "The color of the coat depends on the level of competition," says Alison. "If it's an international competition, or if I'm riding on the United States Equestrian Team, then I have a red coat that I wear. It's got the U.S.A. emblem on it. Every other day I just wear a navy blue coat, or maybe dark green." Alison's outfits don't reflect her style or individual tastes, per se, because they're closer to a uniform.

Alison says the only things she finds truly beautiful are — well, you can have one guess. "I don't use that word a lot, to be honest," she says. "I think I use it the most when I see a horse jump in perfect form. That's beautiful."

The best beauty tricks I've learned: The less, the better.

My deep, dark beauty secret: A good night's sleep.

I can't live without my: Horses.

My favorite homemade beauty concoction: 1) Drink glass of milk daily. 2) Drink plenty of water.

THINGS I INHERITED I WISH I HADN'T/THINGS I INHERITED AND LOVE: I WISH I HADN'T INHERITED MY BIG FEET. I'M GLAD I INHERITED THE ABILITY TO SLEEP ANYWHERE, ANYTIME.

When she was a freshman in high school,

Alison Folland signed up for a drama class so she could get a waiver from sports. Her shining moment: as a chorus member in that season's production of *Evita*. Not long after, her drama teacher sent her down the street to a local casting agency. (An agent had called the school looking for, as Alison puts it, "a sort of overweight girl.") She went to the audition, but the minute she walked into the waiting room, she thought she didn't have a prayer. "Everyone in the waiting room was, like, obese," she says, "and I was like, 'I'm not what I'm supposed to be.'" Luckily for Alison, she came as she was: an admittedly heavy girl who had gone "crazy with the liquid eyeliner – I looked like I was  Uncle Fester. They thought I had dressed up for them. They were like, 'Is this a costume?' I was like, 'Uh, no. I just came from school.'" She got the part.

Alison spent the next few months in Toronto shooting *To Die For*, in which she played an "overweight, insecure" trailer-park teenager who becomes obsessed with Nicole Kidman's character, a local TV personality who herself is obsessed with getting famous. She had never really acted before, but everyone who saw the movie was blown away by Alison, who managed to make her character sweet and likable rather than a two-dimensional joke. Alison herself, though, had a hard time watching it. "I didn't like the way I looked in *To Die For*," she says. "It looked like me on a bad day. But my friends were a lot more shocked than I was. They were like, 'Ali, you were fat in that movie!'" She pauses. "I remember, there was one shot, where I was at this desk at school, and I was pushing my chin down under my hands so my cheeks were kind of like – you know how you push your cheeks up with your fists?" she asks. "My face just looked so large, it was taking up the whole screen, and I was just like, 'Oh my God!'"

Alison Folland

Actress
17 years old
Born and lives in Massachusetts, U.S.A.

My favorite homemade beauty concoction: A bowl of ice cream every day for a slim figure.

WHEN I FEEL THE MOST/LEAST BEAUTIFUL: I FELT THE MOST BEAUTIFUL AT THE PROM. AND WHENEVER I'M IN A WARM CLIMATE. I FEEL LEAST BEAUTIFUL IN THE WINTERTIME WHEN MY SKIN CRACKS.

When she was younger, Alison used to camouflage her figure in what she calls "big, baggy, ugly men's pants. Because when I was younger . . ." She pauses. "I felt very, very self-conscious leaving the house. Sometimes I'd wear bodysuits and stuff, but I felt really weird in tight clothes. When I was 15, or 16 – for a long time I grappled with that. I just have these massive breasts, and I was, like, so self-conscious of them. I just couldn't really wear anything that showed off my body – I didn't hate it, but I was just so aware of it all the time, and wearing tight clothes just made me feel more aware of it."

Adding to her complex was an older sister, now 21, who was a ballet dancer. "You know how ballet dancers are all bone?" she asks. "When I was little, I was very, very large. And I remember coming to New York to visit my sister at the School of American Ballet, and . . ." she says laughing. "I would just feel like such an elephant. I would get very bitter toward her. When I was younger, before I really knew my sister that well, I had this picture of her being the parents' angel, the teacher's angel. We'd be at the dinner table, and I remember watching her eat. She would pick up things,

CLOCKWISE FROM TOP LEFT: ALISON TODAY, BY CB; AT ONE DAY OLD WITH HER DAD AND SISTER SARAH, AGE FOUR; BY CB; WITH HER PARENTS AT HER CONFIRMATION AT AGE 14; BY CB; AT AGE FIVE WITH HER KITTEN RAISIN. RIGHT: DRAWING BY ALISON.

I FREAK OUT IF I LEAVE HOME WITHOUT MY: BRAIN; PAGER.

My deep, dark beauty secret: I keep my hair clean.

CLOCKWISE FROM TOP LEFT: ALISON TODAY, BY CB; WITH HER MOM AND SISTER ON THE DAY OF HER BAPTISM AT AGE ONE; BY CB; WITH HER COUSIN GURU DEV KAUR AT AGE TWO; BY CB; WITH HER COUSIN CHRISTOPHER AT AGE TWO.

and break them in half, into little crumbs, and demurely put them in her mouth and chew them up. She'd eat like one-quarter of what she had on the plate, blah blah blah. It just added to this whole picture I had of her." Alison's sister eventually quit ballet, though, and once Alison got older – "when I started talking to her" – she realized there wasn't much to envy. "She was trapped in this pretty f-✱ed-up world of ballet. They really reward you when you lose weight. I mean, disciplining your body to do these things it's not supposed to do, and not eating to get that certain look." Now her sister is a modern dancer, and Alison is totally relieved. "Now she can let her body basically do what it's supposed to do, you know – grow muscles ✱ the way they're supposed to grow."

As for herself, Alison says she's lost a lot of weight since she's started rowing at school, and thinks that her hormones have leveled off – "my breasts shrunk," she says. Now she feels comfortable wearing "tighter things." But really, her style hasn't changed all that much. "My clothes are usually dirty, my hair is usually dirty – I don't know," she says. "In the summer I have a uniform: jeans and a 'wife-beater,' which is a little red tank top, or something. It's not that I don't like looking good. I just really don't have time to spend on it. Clothes are just a pain – I don't go shopping a whole lot. My style is not something you're going to find on, like, a fashion magazine page – it's just a confluence of things."

Alison Folland

As for makeup, she hardly ever wears any. When she does, it's just eyeliner and lipstick. "If I'm getting dressed up," Alison says, "or if I really feel like looking nice or whatever, I'll wear lipstick. I like big, defined lips." And her mom waxes Alison's eyebrows and upper lip (she runs a small, Sunday-afternoon waxing business out of the house). But that's the only style contribution Alison's mom has made to her look. "Mom's got no style," she says, laughing. "She walks downstairs 🏃 in, like, a T-shirt with a braided belt over it. Do you know that look? I'm like, 'Oh my God, Mom, go back upstairs!' And she's just got this weird layered haircut. She's just got no style at all."

Even though Alison doesn't put much thought or effort into the way she looks, her job makes it very difficult for her to ignore what she otherwise considers superficial. Since *To Die For,* she's done two other movies – she had a bit part in *Before and After* as Edward Furlong's girlfriend, and she has the lead in a movie called *All Over Me,* which just wrapped. "I think my irregularities – and that's according to whoever – have gotten me where I am," she says. "I mean, I think I'm

attractive, but I'm not Hollywood Pretty. And a lot of young actresses are just whores to the Hollywood beauty standard. It's really f-🌀ed up." And, as she points out, even other successful actresses her age are constantly slogged by the media and their peers over the way they look. "I remember reading something about Alicia Silverstone gaining weight or something, and it's just so ridiculous," she sighs. "Look at Claire Danes! The way she looks – she's distinctive. She's not the girl that plays Bimbo #3, but people cutting down her appearance or whatever . . . I don't know, but she's definitely getting the last laugh."

Alison adds, "In some of my heaviest times, when people would probably think that I would be self-conscious, I felt completely comfortable. I had no problem whatsoever. Sometimes I wish this was different or that was different, but, like – I don't know what I am if I can't be proud of who I am. You know?" 🌀

BEAUTY TRICK I'VE LEARNED: DON'T APPLY EYELINER AT A STOPLIGHT.

CB

CB

A FAVORITE DRAWING, BY EGON SCHIELE

KIDDING AROUND AT AGE FOUR

CB

AT AGE FOUR WITH SISTER SARAH, AGE EIGHT

Anoushka

As a young sitar player who also happens to be female, 15-year-old Anoushka Shankar is quite famous in her native India. Anoushka was born in London and lived there with her mom until she was seven. Her father, Ravi, would visit often, but her parents weren't married so she was never sure that he was actually her dad. "But it wasn't an issue for me," she insists. "I didn't know about sex and stuff like that, so I didn't know why he would really be my dad!" But when her parents decided to get married, "They also changed my last name, so I was like, 'Oh, he's really my dad.'"

She then went to live with her parents in India for three years. Now they live in a big, rambling house in Encinitas, California, where she goes to school and takes sitar lessons from her 75-year-old father – who is also her guru. "One's relationship with a guru goes back hundreds of years in India," she says. "It's much more serious than with a teacher, because that's more, you know, an hour a week at a fixed price. But with a guru, it's a lifelong commitment, and usually students will come and live with the guru at his house and be taught by him for years. A guru is traditionally almost like God, because he is a very, very high person in your esteem. It's like a father – and he happens to truly be mine."

Anoushka began playing the sitar seriously when she was 12. "It's probably one of the most difficult instruments to play," she says, "because it's got one of the longest fingerboards, and you have to cover so much space with your hands. And you hold it diagonally, and it's really a pain for your arm – you just go up and down, you know. And over time your back gets messed up because of the way you sit. My dad has 30% scoliosis, and I have 3%. But visually it's a very, very beautiful instrument, because it has so much artwork on it. I love that. And it's got a really, really sweet sound to it, which I like. I truly adore Indian music – it's so beautiful and it really, really touches me."

Anoushka Shankar

Sitarist
15 years old
Born in London, England
Lives in California, U.S.A.
and New Delhi, India

I wash my hair: Every two to three days. If I wash it every day it's too thick. Similarly, after about three days it falls flat. It really just depends on where I am and the weather and climate of the place.

My deep, dark beauty secret: Concealer under my eyes and white eyeliner on the inside rim if I look tired.

SOMETHING I INHERITED I WISH I HADN'T: MY MOTHER'S FEET . THEY'RE REALLY UGLY AND MY SECOND TOE IS WAY LONGER THAN MY FIRST, AND THERE'S A BONE ON THE SIDE THAT STICKS OUT.

MY BIGGEST AS-YET-UNANSWERED BEAUTY QUESTION: WHY SOME PEOPLE FEEL AS IF THEY'D DIE IF THEY LEFT HOME WITHOUT MAKEUP ON. SURE, I WEAR LOTS, BUT I UNDERSTAND THAT IT ONLY ENHANCES MY FEATURES. IF I'M BEAUTIFUL OR UGLY, I WILL BE SO WITH OR WITHOUT MAKEUP.

When she performs with her father, Anoushka wears a traditional Indian outfit called *shalwar kameez.* "It's kind of like a pair of pants and a really long shirt-tunic type of thing – it can be really fancy or really casual depending on how expensive it is," she says. "I generally wear those on-stage, because they're more comfortable than a sari. A sari's a six-yard piece of cloth, and you're wearing a floor-length petticoat from the waist underneath, and a short blouse. What you do is wrap the sari around your waist I think twice, and then you take the other end of it and put it over your shoulder so it hangs, and there are pleats on the front part of it. So even if I pin it, I just have this feeling that it's going to fall off at any second!

"One thing I've noticed," she continues, "is that it's better to play up my youth for music, because it's more admired that way. It's more of a big deal for a 13-year-old to be playing something really complicated than it is for a 30-year-old. I don't know why that works, but that's just the way it is for people. It makes more of an impression. For example, I know dark lipstick makes me look way older, so I avoid that, because I want people to know I'm young."

But when she's in school, Anoushka goes crazy with the makeup. "I wear a lot of *makeup* makeup," she says. She likes Prescriptives the best and is an ardent fan of their color printing system. "They separate the skin tones into yellow-orange, blue-red, and red, and from there they have all these different color schemes that fit your natural color, and it's all separated. So you can just go to your color – mine's yellow-orange – and know what's going to suit you." She hates foundation and opts instead for a light dusting of powder. But Anoushka concentrates most heavily on her eyes. "Some days I may do eye shadow and liquid liner and mascara, or I'll just wear liquid liner or eye shadow or pencil liner," she says. "And lipsticks I prefer to wear looking shiny and clear if I do heavy eye makeup. One makeup artist taught me how to contour your crease and highlight your brow bone – you put the medium colors on your lid and dark on the crease, and maybe shade underneath a little bit."

She thinks her affinity for the eyes has a lot to do with traditional Indian notions of beauty. "If you look at old paintings and things," says Anoushka, "the eyes are always extended, and they wear a lot of heavy black makeup. So I can get away with a lot of eye makeup there – like, a lot of black liquid liner and stuff. But not crazy." What's crazy?

My favorite homemade beauty concoction: There's one Indian wonder my mom makes for me. You mix one tablespoon of "flour" (we use a lentil powder called "Besan" that we buy at Indian stores) with a pinch of turmeric. Then add enough boiled and cooled milk to make a paste. If you have oily skin you can add a few drops of lemon juice also. Mix all together and apply to the face and let dry as a mask, or use as a face wash (it's good on hands and feet too!). It really cleans and smoothes out your skin. The milk moisturizes while the turmeric has great healing qualities and is good for pimples.

CLOCKWISE FROM TOP LEFT: ANOUSHKA AT AGE SEVEN WITH AN ADOPTED DOG IN INDIA; AGE SEVEN; AGE TWO; LEARNING TO DANCE IN INDIA AT AGE SEVEN; WITH HER PARENTS AND CAT IN CALIFORNIA AT AGE 13; WITH HER BEST FRIEND BECCA, BY CB, 1996.

AGE FOUR

How long it takes me to get ready for school: Anywhere from 30 to 75 minutes. One day I wore a sari to school and that took a really long time to put on. On days that I feel like blow-drying my hair straight I take a long time. Usually, I take a really hot shower first, then proceed to decide on what to wear. I can spend anything from five to 20 minutes doing my makeup. Five minutes for breakfast.

I FEEL THE MOST BEAUTIFUL: DURING MY CONCERTS, SINCE IT IS FOR THEM THAT I SPEND THE MOST TIME GETTING READY. IT CAN TAKE UP TO 45 MINUTES JUST FOR MY MAKEUP! THEN I GET READY QUICKLY AND WARM UP FOR A WHILE BEFORE GOING ON-STAGE. HERE GOES: DAB ON CONCEALER UNDER.MY EYES. USE CLINIQUE TOUCH BASE FOR EYES ON MY LIDS - IT HELPS EYE SHADOW STAY ON LONGER. PUT ON LOTS OF LOOSE POWDER, AND DUST OFF EXCESS WITH A POWDER BRUSH. PUT ON BOLD BLACK LIQUID LINER ON TOP EYELID AND UNDER BOTTOM LASHES, THEN EYE SHADOW. I CURL MY TOP LASHES (I DON'T DO THIS OFTEN BECAUSE MINE ARE ALREADY QUITE CURLY). A FEW COATS OF BLACK MASCARA. BLUSH ON THE APPLES OF MY CHEEKS (OR I LOOK LIKE A GHOST ON THE STAGE). THIN LINE OF LIPLINER, THEN LIPSTICK, WHICH I BLOT AND REAPPLY SEVERAL TIMES. ALSO, ON STAGE I'M DOING SOMETHING I REALLY LOVE, AND I'M SURE IT SHOWS. BASICALLY, I FEEL BEAUTIFUL WHENEVER I'M REALLY HAPPY.

IF YOU GAVE ME $100 TO SPEND ON BEAUTY EXCITEMENT, I'D BUY: LOTS OF CHANEL NAIL POLISH, AND LOTS OF LIPSTICKS, LIP PENCILS, AND EYE STUFF OF VARIOUS BRANDS. I USED TO USE PRESCRIPTIVES LOOSE POWDER AND IT'S GREAT, BUT SO IS MAYBELLINE AND IT'S ONE-SEVENTH THE PRICE!

WITH HER DAD AT 22 MONTHS

"Paint a flame over my eye," she says nonchalantly. "I do that at school – I do them in blue actually. I just draw a flame, and then I color it in with eyeshadow. Or you can do it in black – it's totally normal, because we have so many goths at school."

Her makeup, she says, depends on her clothes, which in turn hinge on her moods. "One day I'll wear tight hipsters and a tight shirt, and the next day I'll wear all black and black makeup and black lipstick, and the next day I'll wear something hippie." She's also shown up for class in a sari, and even in her pajamas. "Clothes and makeup are a form of expression of yourself," she says, "and that's also the way people view you. So I just do whatever comes to mind, really." But again, in India, Anoushka must conform to societal standards. "It's nothing like the Middle East," she explains, "but you can't wear things too revealing, because it's not very respectable, and it's shocking to a lot of people. If someone wears shorts there, it creates a big scene. You should wear, you know, long things, nothing sleeveless."

Anoushka says she really has no problem with the Indian style of dress for women, because even when she was living in London her mother raised her with a strong sense of Indian traditionalism. But that's not to say she doesn't clash with her parents over things most American teenagers take for granted. "We used to have a lot of fights about my miniskirts and my spaghetti straps and stuff like that," she admits. "Finally, I just said, 'Listen, I'm not wearing these clothes to try to be somebody. These are just clothes I like and that I'm comfortable in. They are my form of expression.' So they're cool with it."

Another thing: She's not allowed to date. "They don't like the concept of it," she says. "For someone to come and pick me up, take me out, dah-dah-dah, I would have to be older." And yet, on the other hand, Anoushka's dad is her guru – something that, for a female, is still an anomaly in Indian society. "In traditional India," she begins, "some gurus don't even want to teach their own daughters, just because they're female. And it's such an important thing for him to be teaching me. He wants to give me everything he has in music before he dies – this is the only thing he has. He always tells me that if I take

I freak out if I leave home without my: Clinique eye makeup solvent - it's gentle and very effective. Freeman's Dewberry and Peppermint facial toner - it does a miraculous job of removing any dirt or makeup left behind after I wash my face, and it doesn't dry out my skin. Clearasil - even when I'm not broken out I apply a little bit to the sides of my nose and temples, just in case. Also, Sebastian Laminates shampoo and conditioner.

OPPOSITE PAGE AND LEFT: ANOUSHKA THE DAY AFTER HER CARNEGIE HALL DEBUT IN 1996, BY CB. ABOVE: WITH BECCA, 1996, BY CB.

it, then through that, I'll get everything." She pauses. "In India, you know, some people consider women inferior. When you get married there, you're a full-time housewife – like, my great-grandmother on my mother's side got married when she was five. Her parents married her off, and she lived with them until she got her period, and then she went to live with her husband. And in many instances, it's still like that today, because once women get married, they have no time to commit to an instrument, to tour and travel and stuff – so if women do learn at all, they generally stop later on." Anoushka thinks that her parents' relative liberalism comes from having lived in the West. "They're pretty modern as well as being traditional," she says. "Neither of them is at all sexist."

As for how India and America have shaped her ideas about beauty, Anoushka says that America has had a far more pervasive and lasting influence – and not necessarily for the better. "In India, none of my friends wear makeup," she says. "They don't really care enough to bother getting up early in the morning to fix their faces. They're completely confident about the way they are. And they prefer full figures more than they do here. There's such a big, ➤ big thing in America about your weight and your body – it's obsessive. I mean, no matter where I go, I'm always hearing girls go, 'Oh my God, I'm too fat, my thighs are too big, my butt's too wobbly.' And I have, on many occasions, said, 'Oh, I wish I didn't weigh as much,' or 'I wish my stomach was flat' – stuff like that." Still, she's careful not to ride herself too hard, and reminds herself of the things she does appreciate about herself. "I love about myself that I

look different and that I have dark skin," she says. "I don't know why, but I'm just glad to be slightly unique in that way. I prefer to be in a minority, because it's easier for me to stand out."

This is what bothers Anoushka about the word *beautiful*: "It really bugs ➤ me if people freak out when I call a man beautiful," she says. "They're like, 'What? Don't you mean handsome?' I'm like, 'No, I don't. I mean beautiful.' Because most people think – they kind of go, yeah, a girl is pretty, like one level. And then the next level is beautiful, and the next level is gorgeous. But it doesn't work that way for me. Beautiful is a totally universal word. I call a girl beautiful more when she seems like a good person. If she's pretty and she has, like, the kind of eyes that say, yeah, she's a deep person, I'll call her beautiful. And it's the same thing for a guy. If he has beautiful eyes or characteristic eyebrows, I'll call him beautiful, you know?

"There is no fixed form of beauty for me," says Anoushka. "I think that roses are beautiful. But I also think that thorns are beautiful, because they kind of ruin the effect of perfection. I'm not too into perfection, because it's kind of impossible to me. I like beautiful things with just maybe something wrong." ❀

Who has taught me about beauty: Of course, first came my mother. I always played with her lipsticks. I pretty much got into makeup on my own, magazines helped. A friend in India had me try liquid liner, and since then I've been hooked. I love using contrasting colors, like blue, violet, or green eye shadow with my brown eyes. Most important, though, I would say my mother instilled in me the knowledge that beauty comes from the inside. No matter how gorgeous or disfigured a person's face is, the inside really comes forward and shines through.

The best beauty tricks I've learned: Use as little foundation as possible and blend. I don't use any; I don't like the feel of it on my skin. Line your lips before applying lipstick so it doesn't bleed. Whether your eyebrows are thick or thin, keep them neat or your eyes don't really show through. Use a medium shadow all over lid, a darker shadow in the crease of the eye to add depth, and a lighter color on the brow bone to highlight, blend. Tissue off the mascara wand before applying mascara for more natural-looking lashes. Most important to me: Be creative. Don't be afraid to try something new or unusual. And for God's sake, don't follow trends just because.

Something I inherited that I love: My mother's hands - they're extremely flexible and I have really long fingers. I like my eyes; they're like my mother's but lighter like my dad's. My hair is a combination, so instead of being crazily curly or unbelievably frizzy, it's wavy. If I want my hair really curly all I have to do is not brush it after washing it. It'll stay really curly until I brush it out.

I can't live without my: Parents, Becca, and a few other friends: Kabir, Nishant, Anees, Ashby in India. And some in Encinitas, California.

CLOCKWISE FROM TOP: ANOUSHKA TODAY, BY CB; TODAY, BY CB; AT AGE EIGHT WITH HER PARENTS IN NEW DELHI; AGE SIX; WITH HER FATHER RECENTLY IN JAIPUR, INDIA (IN THE TURBAN SHOP).

Christie

Christie Woods
Miss Teen USA® 1996
19 years old
Born and lives in Texas, U.S.A.

There are three levels of competition in the Miss Teen U.S.A. pageant: swimsuit, evening gown, and interview. Christie, who at 19 is the reigning Miss Teen U.S.A., makes sure to stress that the interview is really the deciding factor in who gets crowned. 👑 "They're judging how well you talk," she says. "Even guy [judges], they don't care if you're beautiful or not. If you can't talk, if you just go on up there off the top of your head – they're giving you a low score." So I asked Christie if she would do a pageant-like Q&A with me, and she agreed. (By the way, Christie wants you to know that looks are never the most important thing, even in a beauty pageant.)

Why did you enter a beauty pageant? When I was 16, we got something in the mail. It was more of my mom's idea. She thought, Well, you know, you can win a lot of scholarships through it, and that would really help, and you never know if you're going to be good or bad, but you've got to try and see. And there were a lot of neat prizes, including scholarships – that was the biggest incentive. It wasn't the sense of wanting to win a beauty pageant. [Miss Teen U.S.A. 1996 won more than $150,000 in cash and prizes, including a $30,000 employment contract, $10,000 cash plus swimwear from Jantzen, $10,000 cash plus hair-care products from Salon Selectives, $7,500 cash plus a one-year supply of cosmetics from Cover Girl, a $25,000 portrait in oil by "world famous" artist Anthony Gruerio, "a wardrobe of exquisite Zum Zum evening gowns and prom dresses," and $3,500 cash from the Miss Teen U.S.A. scholarship fund. Bauder College in Atlanta, Georgia, offers a two-year scholarship – as long as the winner (A) wants to attend, and (B) pursues a degree in business administration, fashion merchandising, fashion design, or interior design.]

What was your first pageant like? My first pageant was Miss Houston. There were 82 girls, and I was fourth runner-up. I was pretty excited, it being my first pageant. A lot of the girls there, it wasn't their first pageant, and I did better than a lot of them. But I remember telling my mom, "You know, I'm going to go back next year, and I'm going to win." I was that determined. I didn't ever think I would go to Miss Teen U.S.A. But I thought, you know, I could possibly be Miss Texas Teen, or win a scholarship – you win a scholarship with Miss Texas Teen. And I thought, "This could be something that I'm really good at, and a way to pay for college. I want to win next year."

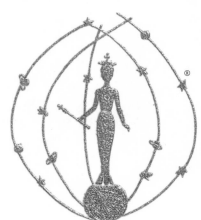

THIS PAGE, CENTER: AT MISS TEXAS TEEN U.S.A. 1996 PAGEANT. COURTESY OF MISS TEXAS TEEN USA™. PHOTO BY GEORGE WONG/ CRYSTAL PRODUCTIONS. BELOW: MISS UNIVERSE LOGO IS A REGISTERED TRADE- AND SERVICE-MARK OF MISS UNIVERSE L.P., LLLP.

I FELT THE MOST BEAUTIFUL: IN MY EVENING GOWN AT THE MISS TEXAS TEEN U.S.A. PAGEANT.

My deep, dark beauty secrets:
1. I make my top lip look thicker with a lipliner.
2. I use an eyebrow pencil to give my eyebrows extra arch.
3. I darken the beauty mark on my right side.

HOW LONG IT TAKES ME TO GET READY FOR SCHOOL: USUALLY 15 MINUTES, AT THE MOST. I DON'T WEAR MAKEUP TO SCHOOL AND I JUST PUT MY HAIR UP IN A PONY-TAIL. I TAKE MY SHOWERS AT NIGHT BECAUSE I LOVE TO SLEEP LONGER IN THE MORNING.

Why do you think you lost Miss Houston Teen? Well, I never worked on the interview part the first year. My question was, "If you won Miss Houston Teen, what would your message be to all the teenagers of the Houston area?" And at the time, I'd never *thought* about something like that. I froze on stage, in front of all those people, for about ten seconds. You know, when you're young like that, you're just worried about what the models are wearing, and what's the latest fashion, and who's dating whom. After that, I really focused on interview questions. Because it's so much more than who is the most beautiful. I mean, you have to go . . . You have to think that . . . In the interview competition, they're judging how well you talk, and they don't care how you look. I've seen guys, and they've scored girls, and if you can't talk, if you can't carry on a conversation, if you don't know what's going on – they don't care if you're beautiful or not. You know, the judges go through a big meeting, are told what to look for, and then "Yes, we would like someone who is nice to look at." It's important, but they don't need someone who is just beautiful. So my sister would just throw off-the-wall questions at me – political, but not too current. "How do you feel about drug abuse? The rising rate of AIDS? Teenage pregnancy?" This did help me. It does. It helps expand your brain. My major is now psychology, because I ponder all the time! I mean, like all the time!

I can't live without my:
1. Oil of Olay shower soap gel.
2. Paul Mitchell shampoo, conditioner, and hair spray.
3. St. Ives Apricot Scrub.
4. Cover Girl "Simply Powder Foundation."

MY BIGGEST AS-YET-UNANSWERED BEAUTY QUESTION: WHY SOME GIRLS HAVE SUCH BEAUTIFUL, CLEAR SKIN — EVEN WITHOUT BASE!

What qualities do you possess that make you a good Miss Teen U.S.A.? I think that any kind of leader, like Miss Teen U.S.A. or Miss Universe, I think you have to be very true to yourself. Don't pretend you're someone you're not. When I meet someone, I think what's good is that I'm a very sincere person and I'm very personable, so that I don't only know how to get along with people who are very wealthy or very poor, or in a very high social status or very low. I can get along with everyone. I don't know, I think . . . I honestly care about people. It feels weird for me to say that to someone I don't even know. But I think that when I have a job like Miss Teen U.S.A., I have that want – that I want to be the best Miss Teen U.S.A. I can be. I want to promote the Rain Forest Gala. I want to promote the Variety Club, which is working with mentally and physically disabled children. Yes, I want to get things to help promote myself, but then also to return and to help promote others.

How do you feel about the swimsuit competition? Umm – I like it! I like both swimsuit and evening gown. I love the evening gown competition because you can't really mess up. You don't have to walk fast, and you have a long gown on so it doesn't matter if you mess up on walking because no one can see your legs. And there's nice music playing. As to the swimsuit competition – I think it's what helped me win my very first pageant. After that I thought, "Oh, well, maybe this is fun." It never really bothered me. I've never been really shy about my body or anything, and so I've never been embarrassed. Plus, after you do

it you think, "Wow, you know, not many people would get in front of an audience and be confident enough to walk around only in a swimsuit and high heels."

But you have to remember that a pageant is about having representatives for teens throughout the United States, being an ambassador for these people. And see, looking nice in a swimsuit shows that you are conscious about your diet, about nutrition, about being physically

WHO HAS TAUGHT ME ABOUT BEAUTY:

1. MAKEUP ARTISTS AT MISS TEEN U.S.A.

2. TV AND MAGAZINES.

fit, and caring about your body, which.is important. That's the importance of the swimsuit competition. Plus, you know, for all pageants, it's entertainment. Pageants are on TV, and they're competing with other 📺 TV shows. I mean, it's not all just about giving a girl a crown. Because it is on TV. And if nobody liked pageants or nobody enjoyed them, then nobody would watch them, and then they wouldn't be on TV, because they would get no ratings.

When did you first think you were pretty? I remember one night I was praying to God. I was just praying to him to make me as beautiful as my sister: "Could I please be as beautiful as my big sister Stacey?" My mom walked in, and she heard, and she said, "Oh but you are, and you're so pretty." Then, always, constantly, she'd say that. You know, when I would come out in a dress – "Oh, you're so pretty!" or "Your hair looks so pretty, Christie." Another thing that really helped was when I turned 16 I got a job as a cashier at a café. I worked with a lot of college students, and for the first time I really got a lot of

Age eight

compliments. And this was right around when I was getting involved in those pageants. So probably around 16 was when I thought, Well, I think I'm pretty. But my looks are not anything that I've ever wanted to rely on in my life – not ever. It's not important to me to be the most beautiful girl in the world or anything like that. I don't want to be a model. But it would be nice to be an actress or something.

How do you prepare for a beauty pageant? I don't know. I mean, I read *Born to Win* and *The Power of Positive Thinking*, and I listened to a ♛ lot of motivational tapes. I think I grew up a lot, I became a different person and a better person when I was getting ready for Miss Teen U.S.A.

When I won Miss Texas Teen, I still didn't know how to wear makeup. I wore foundation, powder, eye-liner, eye shadow, mascara, lipstick – the whole works. I wore it all, and I wore a lot of it. My state directors, after I won Miss Teen U.S.A., said, "You know, of everything, there's one thing we have to work on." I was like, "What?" And they were like, "Your makeup."

How did you feel when they said that? I didn't care. I had just won Miss Teen U.S.A. and I was on top of the world. Nothing could bring me down. They were just letting me know. But I have learned things from different makeup artists. This one guy taught me how to really contour my eyes with eye shadow to open my eyes up and make them look bigger. What I usually do now is, I wear powdered eyeliner because it looks softer, and I apply black eyeliner right by my eyelashes. Then I put a neutral color, like a light pink or a beige, all over my lid. Then I'll get a brown and put it right there in the crease and make it a little wider than the crease. Then I use French Vanilla right under my brow bone, and right above it. If I'm competing in a pageant, then I'll use black mascara. But for everyday purposes, I use a dark brown. Then I usually darken my eyebrows with the mascara wand. I also wax and pluck my eye-brows. What happened was, I saw a girl in real life and then I saw her in her picture, and I thought, Wow! Tasha looks so pretty. Her eyes looked so much bigger in real life, and I wondered why. And then I realized that her eyebrows were arched and waxed in real life, and in her picture they hadn't been. It made *so much* of a difference – it just really opened up her eyes. And I was like, "Wow, this is something I've got to do."

Is there anything about your appearance that you don't like? Well, I sometimes joke about boob jobs and stuff like that. But there are tricks of the trade. You can pad, you can use push-up bras. There are ways to make yourself bigger than you are. ⚲

Did you do any of those things? Mmm-hmm. You do it because everyone else does. You just want to seem proportional to your body. That's what wins swimsuit. You know, when I first got involved, I thought, Oh, there's no way I'll win swimsuit. Because I have no boobs, nothing. But that's not what wins swimsuit. What wins swimsuit is being well-proportioned. So you

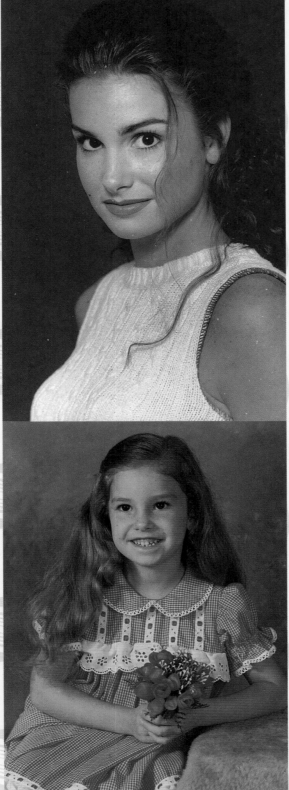

don't want to look like you have bigger boobs than what would be proportional to your body. If you're really thin, you don't make yourself look like you have miles of cleavage.

What do you think of plastic surgery? It's something that's crossed my mind. But honestly, I have friends and family and people who just don't support it, and I don't think I could do it without any support.

How competitive is it at a Miss Teen U.S.A. level? Well, before the pageant, I talked to ♯ Miss Texas. At the time, she told me what it was like when she went to Miss U.S.A., and then the girl, Mandy Jeffries, who crowned me, told me how it was when she went to Miss Teen U.S.A. I knew that it was going to be an emotional roller coaster – I knew that there might be a lot of gossip, a lot of mind-playing games, whatever there is. When you go to Miss Teen U.S.A., you don't need learning experiences anymore. Everyone is there to win. That's what makes it so hard. At some point you have an emotional breakdown – I did. You cry because a lot of things are going on. You're competing and you're there for so long and everyone wants it so bad, but you know that only one person can get it, so it's like you cry that one time to come to terms with it. But just once. You feel better after that!

Christie, what do you think is the biggest problem facing America's youth? There are so many problems actually facing teens. One thing I have focused on is the rising rate of teenage pregnancy and AIDS among teenagers in the United States. I think this is a big problem. Teenage sexuality is just a problem in the United States. It affects you and me.

Welfare, you know? Taxes. I mean, what's going on? Half of this welfare is going to unwed teenage pregnant girls, you know, and their babies. I did a project on this, and when I first started the speech for it, I was going to write, you know, abstinence is the only way. Then I started reading more about it . . . I do believe in mandatory sex education classes. I think abstinence is the number-one safest and most moral choice, but I mean, look at the statistics. Not everyone is choosing abstinence. The reality is that's not the only choice out there to be made, and not every teenager is going to make it. So when they decide to go the other way, they need to know how to protect themselves and what's going on. There's a sense of "I don't give a care," and I don't think that's a good way to feel. I think that's what leads to gang violence and teenage pregnancy. And because my major is psychology, it's not like I just want to know what the problem is – I want to know what's causing the problem. My friends would probably describe me as analytical. They would say that I analyze things a lot.

So if you analyze yourself, why would you say you enter beauty pageants? I would say to prove to myself that I am a winner. To prove to other people that I am a winner . . . I don't know. I've never sat down and thought about that. It was like . . . I just wanted to . . . I don't know exactly. ❁

Christina Ricci

Actress

17 years old

Born in California,
lives in New York, U.S.A.

I am trying everything I can think of to get them to give me the back booth at Time Café, even though there will only be two of us. But the waiters – who aren't really all that attitudinal, even though it's a downtown New York City restaurant – are insisting they have to hold it for parties of four or more, blah-blah-blah. Then my date, Christina Ricci, walks up. "How are you?" "We haven't seen you in a while!" "Where would you like to sit?" They can't do enough for her. "Do you think we could have, um, the back booth?" I ask. They nod solicitously and quickly usher us over. And then our menu-studying is interrupted by a constant stream of cute waiters who all stop by to ask if she's being taken care of. All of this pseudo-calm buzzing around her strikes me as a bit odd because, even though she's a famous actress and all, she easily blends into a crowd and does absolutely nothing to draw attention to herself: She's tiny, with a pale face totally devoid of makeup, and she's wearing an old pair of beat-up blue jeans and a dark blue leather jacket – an item she picked up at a thrift store in Spanish Harlem where clothes go for $10 a pound. As the fifth or so waiter completes a drive-by greeting to Christina, I shoot her a quizzical look. "My mom and I used to be in here all the time last year," she explains. "We don't cook, so we would come in here every night really early, at 5:00. But now I've started to go out during the week, so we don't have dinner as much together." She shrugs slightly.

Christina just finished making a movie called *Ice Storm,* in which she plays the eldest daughter of alcoholic, seriously dysfunctional parents (played by Kevin Kline and Joan Allen). She also did a short film, for a director friend, based on a very early, very dark version of "Little Red Riding Hood." But she's decided to take a break from work. "I haven't done anything since then and I don't think I'm doing anything for a while," she says nonchalantly, then adds, "I'm doing my college applications."

BY FRANK OCKENFELS

WHO HAS TAUGHT ME ABOUT BEAUTY: SADLY, SOCIETY. MY PERCEPTIONS HAVE BEEN, UNFORTUNATELY, TYPICALLY MISCONSTRUED.

Plus, she says, she's psyched to have a rest from auditioning constantly. ✋ Even though she's practically a veteran actress at 17 (she was Winona Ryder's little sister in *Mermaids*, Wednesday Addams in both Addams Family movies, and one of the four stars of *Now and Then*), Christina says the whole process is incredibly stressful and often demoralizing. "When I was little," she says, "I was like, 'All right, this is fun.' And now I'm like, 'Get me out of this hell.' I mean, acting always feels right to me, and I was taught never to doubt my ability, that I'm good, so I always feel that according to me, I did it right," she says matter-of-factly. "But whenever I don't get a part, I immediately think it's because I'm not pretty enough." I'm shocked that this is an issue for Christina, especially when it so obviously could not be the case. But she insists. "On auditions they'll say something like – I don't know. Ever since I was really little, people would go, 'No, she's too healthy.'" I ask her what exactly that means. "Cause I was a pudgy child, a roly-poly kid," she answers, as she happily munches on some bread. Christina says she was nine years old the first time she heard that. (But I'm thrilled to report that, when it's time to order, Christina asks for a plate full of fish and veggies without hesitation.)

It's hard not to take the rejection personally, she says, because not all auditions consist of actually reading for the part. Sometimes directors and casting agents just

want to meet with her, see what she looks like, and have some small talk. "I have such a hard time because I get so nervous – I turn bright red and I shake and stuff," she admits. "One of the things I don't like about acting is that I really feel judged all the time, and that bothers me. Because it makes you paranoid. It makes you think that everyone's judging you, and most people really don't care. But it's so scary," she continues, wide-eyed. "I have this friend who's a producer – who worked for Universal – and the things he would

tell me that went on! Like how they would take the videos of all the screen tests back to all the executives. I was like, 'I don't want to hear this.' They take people apart so crazily – they're almost like a bunch of catty women at the gym. I feel like I don't want to imagine that this happens with my audition tapes." But she's quick to reassure me that she deals with disappointment fairly well. "When it's a part I really wanted and I didn't get it, yeah, I'm devastated," Christina admits. (She auditioned for *Romeo & Juliet*, but

ABOVE: At age eight. Opposite page, top: Age one; bottom: age five.

MY DEEP, DARK BEAUTY SECRET: I SOMETIMES WASH MY FACE WITH DISHWASHING LIQUID. MY SKIN TENDS TO BE OILY SO EVERY ONCE IN A WHILE IT'S REALLY GOOD AND DRYING. USING IT TOO OFTEN IS WAY TOO DRYING THOUGH.

obviously didn't get the part. She got the part in *Ice Storm* when Natalie Portman's parents decided they didn't want their daughter playing the role; Christina's agent convinced the director that she should have a shot.) "So I go for a walk and I visualize tearing the director and the casting director apart, limb by limb." She laughs loudly. "And then I feel better."

Even though Christina loves acting enough to put up with the requisite blows to her self-esteem, I'm still curious to know exactly what it is about her appearance she doesn't like. "I don't think that I'm ugly," she responds quickly. "There's nothing repulsive about my features. But I think that the problem I have with my looks is that I know I'm never going to be perfect – like, I don't like my huge nose, for example. And, to me, beauty and perfection are in one part of my mind, even though I don't really believe that they're the same thing. But in the part of my mind that totally lays down to society and reads the fashion magazines and wants to be accepted . . . I know I'm never going to be that."

Yet, in terms of other people, Christina's definition of beauty is pretty elastic. 🐾 "I really feel that something or someone who is beau-

tiful makes you feel a certain way when you see them," she says. "Not just, like, sexually, but really makes you feel something. And I think that your face is totally a projection of who you are, and that's what makes you feel a certain way – the way

people are reflections of themselves through their eyes or through the way they smile or something. Like, I was thinking about this today – I always end up with ugly guys." She giggles slightly. "What do you mean?" I ask. "Guys that aren't really like –" She looks up at the ceiling. "You know, they're not cute. But there's always something about

them. And you meet people like that, like, they smile or something, and I go, 'Oh my God, that person's beautiful.' I mean," she continues, "I've learned. I've met so many people who are supposed to be gorgeous. And so many people who are supposed to be ugly."

Christina's not seeing anybody right now. Between work and school she's been super-busy. She attends the Professional Children's School in Manhattan, which she loves, she says, because "everyone is really nice – like polite. Whereas in normal high school there's a lot of undisguised hatred 🐾 and fights and stuff." I'm surprised, I tell her, because it seems like there would be a lot of competition for jobs when all of your classmates are performers, but Christina tells me no, that she had a worse time of it in regular school. "When I was little and first started acting," she says, "I would come back to school and talk about it a lot. And that didn't work at all because people did get jealous. They felt that I thought my life was so much better and more exciting than theirs. So I never talk about it," she says resolutely. "Ever. And even now, around kids or my peers, if they talk about someone that I've met or I know and they say something not true, I don't say anything.

My biggest as-yet-unanswered beauty question: How on earth do people get that constantly cocked eyebrow thing going?

And I think because of that, people don't get jealous because I'm not throwing it in their faces all the time. I allow them to forget. Plus," she adds, "I dress like such a slob. I always look so normal, and I can't stand people not liking me, so I always make sure that if they don't like me or that maybe they're jealous of me, I do something to make them see that they shouldn't be."

times in the car be . . . nd she always gets away. It's . . . zing." She looks down at her glass and twists her fork through her fingers. "Actually, it's really awful," she says, "but I get jealous sometimes. I don't really look like my mom, obviously, I look more like my father. And I would always notice people looking at me and looking at her, looking at me and looking at her. Or people

BY DAVID SEIDNER

I FREAK OUT IF I LEAVE HOME WITHOUT MY: HAIR DRYER - WITHOUT IT MY HAIR IS EXTREMELY SCHIZOPHRENIC.

Maybe part of the reason she's so attuned to other people's resentment is because Christina herself gets jealous when comparing herself to the way other people look — particularly her mother. "I think my mom's beautiful," says Christina. "She's never gotten a ticket in her life! 🛥 She's been stopped five

saying, 'Gee, you don't really look alike at all,' and in the same breath saying, 'Oh, your mom's so beautiful.' You know? So yes, it's really hard. Sometimes I just don't want to go out with her because I look like a slob and she looks nice and pretty, but at the same time, I like that she's really beautiful and that peo-

Chapstick." She scrapes up the remnants of her fish and scoops them into her mouth. "I mean, I always try to make my face look pretty, and sometimes I'll dress up. I look nice when I wear my skirt and a little T-shirt. Then I look nice." Yet Christina can only deal with casual, thrown-together attractiveness. She tells me that she's petrified about going to her prom because of the intense beauty pressure. "You have to wear a nice dress!" she exclaims. "And I really want to wear a dress and look really pretty, and I just know I'm going to fail. I always think it's too scary and risky to try and look nice because if you fail miserably, it's so much worse than if you didn't even try."

As we settle the check and start gathering our stuff to head out, Christina debates the pros and cons of going to the prom out loud, like she's having a conversation with herself. Then she turns to me and says firmly, "You know, I should go. I love dancing, and then there'll be an afterparty, and I want to organize a really big breakfast and invite my whole school, everyone I know." She beams. "And I want to go out in a limo and wear a really nice dress. And look really pretty." ❀

ple are amazed with her because she's so pretty." She pauses, then adds, "She's taller than I am and fairer than I am, but if you look closely at the both of us, we do look alike."

The weird thing about Christina is that she totally looks her age (maybe because she's so tiny), but she talks way older than 17. She can spend one weekend hanging out with her pals from school, staying up late smoking cigarettes, and the next weekend out with people twice her age — actors, makeup artists, producers, writers, me. "It's just bizarre," says Christina. "I feel like I'm 18 and I feel like I am an adult, but I'm so

mad because I really, really, really liked being a little kid. I loved it so much," she says quietly, "that it's really upsetting me a little."

And even though she's picking up on subtle changes – like, her mom doesn't give it to her if she misses curfew anymore – Christina says it's hard to feel older when she still looks like a kid. "I mean, I always wear makeup," she says, "because I feel strange without it. Like, I'll wear eyeliner and mascara and pencil, but I can't stand wearing lipstick. I look like a clown. I'll put it on and people will go, 'Why is that little girl wearing lipstick?' So I wipe it off and just wear cherry

THE BEST BEAUTY TRICKS I'VE LEARNED: HOLD MASCARA TO BASE OF EYELASHES AND SORT OF BLINK GENTLY BEFORE RUNNING IT ALONG THE REST OF THE EYELASHES. ALSO, LETTING ONE COAT OF MASCARA DRY THEN APPLYING OTHERS.

When she was five months old,

Dominique Moceanu's father, Dimitry, hung her up by her fists on the clothesline in the family backyard. He wanted to see how strong she was; she was already thinking that she might have the future in gymnastics that he, as a teenager, was forced to relinquish. Dominique hung on until the clothesline snapped, and her father caught her. Question answered.

Today, at 15, Dominique is a world-class gymnast. Most of you probably remember her from the 1996 Olympics, when she competed on the U.S. Gymnastics Team; her near-perfect routine, along with Kerri Strug's (who we all know competed in spite of a badly injured ankle), helped win the gold medal. Dominique herself was performing at a disadvantage. "I had a stress fracture in my shin at the Olympics," she tells me, "and that was very painful. For a while I didn't know if I could go. I was scared, I was worried because I couldn't work out. I knew I could do it mentally, but my body wouldn't let me."

The stress fracture wasn't the result of a bad fall or a single incident. As she puts it, "There was just so much pounding that my body was taking that it was just falling apart." She started beating herself up emotionally, she tells me. "I was mad at myself, like, how could I let this happen? Why did it happen? It picked a perfect time to just, you know, happen." She says that her parents – both Romanian immigrants who moved to the United States so Dominique could train with fellow Romanian Bela Karolyi – gave her lots of support. "They were worried," she says today, "but they knew I was strong enough, and that I could make it through." Dominique adds that while it was great that the team won the gold, "I just wish I could have done better myself."

Dominique has been in training for the Olympics since she was three-and-a-half years old. A typical day for her would be to get up at 7:00 a.m., go to the gym for three hours, go home for lunch and schoolwork, head back to the gym at around 4:00, practice for three more hours, then go back home, eat dinner, and fall into bed. She insists that gymnastics is something she's always loved, but then begins to tell me about the stuff she hasn't loved so much. Like, by the time she was nine years old she had lived in California, Chicago, Florida, and finally Houston, to be where the best coaches were. How she would get sick of training all the time and having to be so rigidly focused on a single point to the exclusion of everything else. "You see all your friends out there," Dominique says, "and they're all having fun and going to parties, and you want to go, too, but you're stuck in the gym every day." And, most important, what gymnastics has done to her body.

"Since the Olympics," she tells me, "I've been taking it easier. Because my body needs a break. I've put it through a lot. I mean, before the Olympics and during the 11 and a half years I've been training, I put it through a lot of stress and a lot of things that normal teenagers wouldn't really put it through. But," she adds, "my body has held up really well. I have good physical therapy every day. I try to take care of it as much as I can so it won't get any worse."

This reminds me of the debate that was raging last summer over whether girls on the cusp of adolescence should be putting their bodies through so much strain; many gymnasts don't grow at a normal rate, and don't begin menstruating when they should. And since then, the Olympic Committee decided to raise the minimum

Dominique Moceanu

Gymnast
15 years old
Born in California,
lives in Texas, U.S.A.

age for young women gymnasts. Now they must be at least 16, not 14, to compete. Dominique herself was only 4'6" at the Olympics, but has grown two-and-a-half inches since. She's also gained weight; now she's 80 pounds as opposed to last summer's 70. When I ask Dominique if she thinks competitive gymnastics is damaging in any way, she adamantly disagrees. "In all other sports, you have to watch your weight, too," she says. "I guess people see little kids, and they think of gymnastics as, you know, deteriorating our bodies and messing us up. But I don't think gymnastics has caused anybody . . ." She sighs. "It's just that some people have different opinions." Still, she tells me, the major reason she's taking a break is because she can feel her body changing and wants to leave it alone for a while. "I'm, like, really happy I've grown," says Dominique. "But it was pretty hard at first – your body starts maturing and things start getting weird and you start feeling different things, and it's awkward sometimes. You start, you know . . . when you eat normal things, you start to feel a little bit more swollen or bloated." I ask her what she means by "normal things," and she explains that when she was training, she had to adhere to a strict diet of fruits, vegetables, and small portions of things like grilled chicken breast. Now she can go a little crazy, and she's liking it.

Dominique says that getting to the Olympics has always been her dream; that she wouldn't go back and change a thing; that gymnastics has given her "a lot of discipline, and it's made me a better, stronger person – all the hard times and all the injuries have made me tougher and stronger mentally." But, for now, she's having fun slacking off. "I get to do things with my friends and go out and actually be with them," she says excitedly. "It's really fun for me, because I never really got to do that before." Meaning go to the movies or eat at McDonald's or just wander aimlessly around the local mall.

Dominique's favorite places to shop are Banana Republic, the Gap, The Limited, and Express. She prefers the preppy look and wears blue jeans almost every day. "We have a dress code at my school, and we have to wear khakis and polo shirts or Oxford shirts, and I really don't mind," she says. "We all look well put together." And unless she's going outside to run a

couple of miles, Dominique always puts on makeup. "I have, you know, a reputation to uphold," she tells me. "I mean, I have pride in myself, and when I walk outside I want people to say, 'Well, she looks nice today.'"

For the most part, Dominique goes for a natural look. "I wear a little, you know, light blush, just to make color on my face," she says. "And I wear eye shadow just to define the eyes out, like a brownish-blond color, a light color. And I just wear a lipliner, you know, a lip-pencil thing to make my lips stand out, and a really neutral-color lipstick." Her favorite makeup brands are Clinique, Maybelline, and L'Oréal.

She picked up the neutral-color palette when she did a photo shoot for *Seventeen* magazine – Dominique says the makeup artist told her to steer clear of anything dark because she's still too young to pull off heavy drama. Plus she's got dark hair and fair skin, so she doesn't really need it. "And I liked how they used a little light purple on my eyes," she says. "That was really pretty. I like to use that once in a while, because it really makes your eyes stand out just a little bit. You can't use too much," she cautions, "just enough."

IF YOU GAVE ME $100 TO SPEND ON BEAUTY EXCITEMENT, I'D BUY:
BLUSH, FACIAL WASH, LIPSTICK, LIP PENCIL, EYE SHADOW.

Dominique tells me that when she did the shoot, she was a little surprised that the photographer told her not to smile. "I love to smile," she says with a laugh. "But they told me just to look serious, because it looks better or something. And when I look at that picture now," she continues, "it looks so different from me. But it's so pretty! I love it, you know? It's a great picture. I mean, the models they [Seventeen] put in there are so beautiful; it's like an honor to be in a magazine."

Even though Dominique is at the opposite end of the fashion magazine spectrum – short, compact, and peppy as opposed to tall, lanky, and sullen – she says she never feels like she doesn't measure up, ✝ or that she needs to conform to one set standard of beauty. "I think it's fine," she says. "A lot of girls have their own style and their own way of doing things, and I like looking at the models and picking up tips. But, I mean, I'm very happy with the way I look, and, you know, who you are has a lot to do with it. I mean, looks are important, but people have to like the person inside. Because I think that every girl has a beauty part of her, you know, which is the best part of her. You've just got to find it in yourself." ◉

When I feel the most/least beautiful: I feel least, when I just finish a workout, and most after I take a shower and get ready to go somewhere.

OPPOSITE PAGE, CLOCKWISE FROM TOP: AT AGE ONE; WITH HER PARENTS, DIMITRY AND CAMELIA, AND SISTER CHRISTINA, IN 1995; AT AGE 10 WITH CHRISTINA. THIS PAGE, CLOCKWISE FROM TOP: BY DAVE BLACK; AGE 11 AT THE 1992 PAN AMERICAN GAMES IN SÃO PAULO, BRAZIL; SKIING RECENTLY.

Filippa

Model
14 years old
Born in Germany
Lives in New York, U.S.A.

It all started a couple of years ago

when Filippa was walking down a New York City street with her cousin, who was visiting from Paris. She noticed a man staring at her, and it made her uneasy. He trailed her for a bit before finally approaching her. "He was like, 'Are you a model?'" recalls Filippa. "And I was like, 'Well, not really.' And he said, 'Well, you should be,' and he showed me his card." The man was actually a photographer scouting for Next, a prestigious New York City modeling agency. Within a couple of months, Filippa was on the cover of *Seventeen* magazine. A few months later, she would catch her own face on the sides of commuter buses. She was 13 years old.

Filippa lives with her two sisters (her older sister, a sometime model, is 17; the little one's 7), her mom (a painter), and her dad (a German diplomat) in a plush Manhattan townhouse near the United Nations. Because of her dad's job, she's lived all over the world: Liberia, Romania, Germany, and Israel. She attends the United Nations School full-time and works only after school and during weekends and vacations. She says that while there are things she likes about modeling – and that it was something she always wanted to do – sometimes she hates it.

In person, Filippa's quite delicate. She can't be more than 5'7" or 5'8" (most models are usually more like 5'10"). And she photographs much older – in pictures, her eyes seem bigger, her features more razor-sharp than fine, her demeanor somewhat defiant. But sitting across from me in her parents' book-lined living room at the end of a school day, she just looks like a 14-year-old girl. She wears absolutely no makeup; the only thing that gives away her double life: an up-to-the-minute, perfectly executed zigzag part through the middle of her scalp.

On her jobs, Filippa is always accompanied by her mother. Sometimes she works from 8:00 in the morning well into the evening. When the preparation seems to take forever Filippa can get frustrated and at times finds herself having to hide her agitation. This is what she thinks most girls don't realize about modeling: "Everybody thinks it's always so much fun and that you're going to be famous. And it's true that a lot of people get to know you, and a lot of people are like, 'Oh my God, you're a model, blah-blah-blah.' But at points I just hate it. If the photographer can't decide how he wants the picture to be, it can take hours for him to decide. And I'm sitting there and waiting and waiting and waiting, and inside I just get nervous and aggravated and everything else. I mean, you just have to deal with it, but I always think, Well, I could be doing something else now. I could be with my friends."

How long it takes me to get ready for school: Get up at 6:45 to take a shower. Do my hair, get it all perfect and smooth. Put all the gel and mousse in it. Get dressed and put on my lipstick which takes me all together like 45 minutes to one hour.

I CAN'T LIVE WITHOUT MY: "FAMILY" COMPANY: EXTRA FOR YOU.

SOMETHING I INHERITED I WISH I HADN'T / THINGS I INHERITED AND LOVE:
• HATE MY BROAD SHOULDERS.
• I WISH I HAD LONGER LEGS.
• THE REST IS ALL GOOD.

I FREAK OUT IF I LEAVE HOME WITHOUT MY:
• FOUR PACKS OF WINTERFRESH 25 CENT GUM.
• MY WALKMAN.
• MY LIPSTICKS.

BY PATRIK ANDERSSON

Getting hair and makeup done on photo shoots takes a couple of hours – at least – and Filippa isn't wild about having her face and hair covered with all kinds of products. "I've gotten used to it now," she says, "but in the beginning I just wanted to go to the sink and wash it all off. I hate makeup – when I put it on my face, it feels like plastic. I hate wearing makeup – except lipstick. That's all I wear. With mascara and everything, I feel like my eyelashes are going to fall out when I take it off." The only other cosmetic she does like is cover-up, but that's only for emergencies. "Just when I have a pimple," she says, "and just on the spot – not, like, *all over* my face."

Filippa also likes to be super-careful about her hair, which is very long. Most stylists tend to go heavy on the mousses and gels and hairpins and teasing, all of which can be harmful to the hair. "I mean, I love the way my hair looks, but sometimes when I get it dyed and treated it gets *so bad*," she groans. "It's not that bad, but I see a lot of models who have hair that looks damaged, you know? Some hairdressers will just dive in and get real nasty." As soon as she finishes a job, she goes home and rinses all the products out.

Filippa has been disappointed by some of her colleagues. "I just don't like some of the models," she says firmly. "I went up to this one girl, and I was like, 'Hi. I'm Filippa.' She went like this" – Filippa holds up her head and quickly darts her eyes up and down, as if she's inspecting me from head to toe – "and she just turned around. That happened to me twice already. And

I was just like, 'Sorry! I didn't mean to upset you or anything.' Models compete with each other a lot," she says matter-of-factly. "I guess some have low self-esteem or low confidence or whatever, but if they don't think . . ." Her voice trails off. "I feel bad for them. Whatever."

Filippa also points out that she has met a lot of nice models, too, and she admits to comparing herself with the others and often feeling inferior. "Most models always wear black, and, like, big boots, really high-heeled boots, and I feel short compared to them. I feel like I'm a little dwarf compared to them. I remember walking into Calvin Klein, and this tall model was walking in front of me. And I felt like I was a delivery guy or something."

Aside from draining schedules and contending with the outsized ego-tripping of some of the other models, her career has given her yet another problem: trouble at school. Even though the kids at her high school are supposedly well-traveled and sophisticated, Filippa's been the object of gossip and envy. "When I first started modeling, a lot of the girls in my grade were like, 'Well, I don't want to be friends with Filippa anymore – she's going to be a bitch.' It was really hard," she says softly. "I got mad. And I'd ask my friends, 'Why are they being like that? I didn't do anything to them.' And they were like, 'Oh, Filippa, don't worry about it, they're just jealous.'" She stops to consider this. "Maybe they were, I don't know. If I would've seen a girl in my grade who was a model, like a real model, I would probably think that she would get really conceited. But I didn't turn into a bitch or nothing." After a while, things calmed down a lot. Even though she still runs into trouble sometimes, Filippa says stuff like that doesn't happen so much anymore, mainly because she's learned how to deal, and her friends realize she hasn't changed. "There's this girl in my grade who used to be a model, and then I started doing modeling and she hated my guts. But then we talked it out, and now she's really nice."

Filippa doesn't dress like a model. She dresses the way most of her friends "from the hip-hop world" dress. Before she got into that scene, she used to wear stuff like bell-bottoms and baby T-shirts, and she'd pull her hair back into pigtails. "Then I just wanted to dress the way

they [the hip-hop crowd] were dressing. I loved the style," she says. "I started wearing big earrings [she's wearing a big pair of gold ones today] and thin chains and hi-top sneakers, or short skirts and boots – you know, just the style." And she likes the boys in that scene, too, although, or maybe because, they've gotten in trouble with the cops a few times for "writing up" (graffiti). (She admits her mom was not psyched about this and that she used to have to lie about where she was and whom she was with, "but now I tell her," she says.) Filippa says these friends are not like the kids at

BY FRANCESCA SORRENTI

school – they think it's cool she's a model. "They don't turn their backs on you or nothing," she says. "One of my boyfriends was like, 'Damn, I don't want everybody knowing my girl!'" She smiles, like she knows he was secretly proud. "It's cool."

Filippa says there are other things about her job that she loves, like getting recognized on the street or seeing herself in magazines. 🐾 And she loves runway. "I

TOP OF PAGE, LEFT TO RIGHT: AT AGE TWO; WITH HER FRIEND KARIMA, 1996; WITH HER SISTERS LISI AND ANNA; WITH HER FAMILY, 1996; GETTING THE CURL RIGHT, 1996; WITH HER SISTER AT AGE TWO; HER FRIEND DALIA.

How long it takes me to get ready for a party:
Take a shower and do hair (30 minutes). Find the right outfit to wear (30 minutes max.).
Lipstick = dark brown liner and light brown inside (10 minutes). Mascara and maybe eyeliner (brown) (15 minutes max.).

love doing shows!" she exclaims. "I love it so much. I think it all has to do with acting, because you're always a different person, and it's like a show. I love the loud music, all the photographers everywhere, people staring at you, all the attention. I love it." And though it might seem like the ultimate in beauty validation – getting paid to look pretty – Filippa says, for her, that barely even registers. "I mean, in the business, whatever. They tell you every second how beautiful you are. And I think, Okay, they're saying that to everybody. I'm not that gullible. I'm not like, 'Oh my God, they think I'm beautiful – I'm beautiful, I'm beautiful!' That's not the way I am." As a matter of fact, Filippa doesn't believe that she's beautiful.

These are people Filippa finds beautiful:

1. Her friend Dalia. "She's so beautiful. She's really gorgeous, and she's really self-confident, and she's one of the sweetest people I know. She's not one of those people that goes around showing off that she's beautiful. And that's why I love her."

2. A model named Laura. "I guess I compare myself with her. I think she's really beautiful. She's 14, and I don't think I'm as attractive. It's weird, because most of the jobs she does, I do the next season. I mean . . . there's, like, a little bit of jealousy in some way."

3. Her other friend Karima. "She thinks she's the ugliest thing in the world. I think she's absolutely gorgeous. She's Russian, and she kind of has Asian eyes. She's really shy around guys. I remember when I first saw her, I didn't think she was all that . . . You know, I thought she was a really cool person, but, I don't know. For me, once I get to know people, their beauty comes

BY FRANCESCA SORRENTI

out, it comes out so fast. I look at them, and I'm like, 'My God, they're so beautiful.' I don't know, it comes from the inside or something."

Filippa says that she feels good "when I feel that I look good, when I like what I'm wearing, I feel happy, and I talk to everybody." And on the whole, she says, she's happy with herself and the way she looks. But when she feels bad about her appearance, she avoids everyone. "Sometimes I wake up and I'm like, 'I hate my hair! It's straight! I want curly hair!' Or, like, sometimes I can't find what I want to wear, and I feel so bad, and I just don't want to get out of bed," she says solemnly. "And, like, I'm so depressed all day, and I'll look at my friend and go, 'Oh God, she's so beautiful, I look really bad next to her.' I never hang out with my friends after school on those days. I just get home as fast as I can and put on my leggings and a shirt or whatever and think, What happened?"

Actually, she has a theory. "In Germany, people don't care about this stuff – like girls and their chests?!" she exclaims. "There was nothing like that. But in New York, everybody's like, 'Big butt, big chest,' you know? 'Curvy butt looks fine.' Here the body just means everything. In Germany, people care about their looks, but not *that much*." Filippa sighs. "I learned all this other stuff when I came here. I learned this in America." ❦

BEAUTY PRODUCT I'D LOVE TO FORGET:
• COVER-UP (MY SKIN IS SUFFOCATING).
• TOO MUCH MASCARA (FEELS LIKE MY EYELASHES ARE GLUED TOGETHER).
• GEL AND MOUSSE (I HATE IT, BUT I LOVE THE WAY IT LOOKS).

IF YOU GAVE ME $100 TO SPEND ON BEAUTY EXCITEMENT, I'D BUY:
• DARK BROWN LIPLINER;
• LIGHT BROWN INSIDE;
• BEAUTIFUL BLACK LONG LASH MASCARA;
• BLACK AND BROWN LIQUID EYELINER;
• LITTLE BLACK STARS I CAN STICK TO THE LEFT
SIDE OF MY LEFT EYE.

TOP OF PAGE, LEFT TO RIGHT: AT AGE 11; HER FRIEND NORA; WITH HER SISTERS LISI AND ANNA; FINISHING TOUCHES ON THE CURL, 1996; AT AGE ONE; FILIPPA TODAY; ON THE BEACH, AGE TWO. BOTTOM, LEFT: BY FRANCESCA SORRENTI; RIGHT: AT AGE FIVE.

BY KELLY KLEIN

Heather Todd

College Student
18 years old
Born in Saskatchewan,
lives in Manitoba, Canada

Even now, four years later, 18-year-old Heather Todd doesn't know why. She remembers how it started, and how she eventually realized she had a problem, but there's lots of stuff in between she can't recall – partly because she suffered memory loss as a result of her illness. "I had no idea what I was getting into," she says today. "But I think maybe if I had, it may have helped."

This is Heather's story.

I would have been 14 when it sort of started. At school they used to weigh people in gym on the first day of school. And that year when I weighed myself, I wasn't happy with what the scale said – 133 pounds. I was 5'4" or 5'5", and I thought that was too heavy. I was just really upset with what it said, and worried that I was going to keep on gaining all that weight and be really, really fat, and ... I don't know, I just felt kind of worthless, I guess.

So first I just started exercising more, a half hour a day, usually in the morning. But that didn't work, because I didn't change my eating habits at all – I'd eat a fair bit of junk food, like chocolate bars and cookies. So when the exercising didn't work, I decided that I would cut out everything that I ate except for one meal a day, which would be supper, so my parents wouldn't notice what I was doing. I also increased my exercise to

more like an hour. I was doing biking and aerobics, and I would also do a lot of sit-ups – about 300 a day – because I was so determined to get a flat stomach. That, to me, signifies being really thin. You see all these ads in magazines, and all the models are always so thin. None of them have stomachs.

Anyway, I was still 133 pounds when I cut out food, and I know in the first three days I lost about five pounds or something. Oh, I was so happy. Like overjoyed, like something had finally been resolved. My goal was 115 pounds. A lot of teenagers I knew in my class were probably somewhere around there, and it just seemed like an okay weight, I guess. It took a few months to get to 115. But I just didn't think I was thin enough. I thought I looked the same that I did when I was 133. So I figured, Well, I've got to keep going.

My friends kind of bugged me to eat and started telling me I was being stupid. They knew I wasn't happy with how I looked and stuff like that. One of them was really worried and kind of went to a teacher when I got down to 115. I was angry because she went behind my back, but also because I thought, Well, my parents are going to find out, and that was about the

IF YOU GAVE ME $100 TO SPEND ON BEAUTY EXCITEMENT, I'D BUY: A FACIAL, MANICURE, PEDICURE.

WHO HAS TAUGHT ME ABOUT BEAUTY: MAGAZINES, FRIENDS, MOM.

Something I inherited I wish I hadn't: My round face.

last thing I wanted. So the teacher tried talking to me, and he alerted the school counselor, who also tried talking to me. They tried to figure out why I was doing it, and where I wanted my weight to be now that I wasn't happy at 115, and also to

important. My grades were good but I always wanted them to be the best, and they weren't the best, and my sister also did pretty well in school, so we were pretty competitive. She's two years older than me. She became quite popular in school. It

who specialized in eating disorders. She'd weigh me and then started threatening to send me to the hospital if I lost any more weight. I still didn't listen and ended up going to the children's hospital. I was there three weeks. Basically, they set a

work on my self-esteem and stuff like that. I said that I wasn't going to stop dieting until I thought I was thin, but I also made it clear that I really didn't want my parents to know, and they respected me for as long as they could.

I would still eat supper unless my parents were out. If they were, I'd make something and then pour it down the Garbarator. Like, the plate would be dirty and everything, and then there would be, like, the smell of food, and I would just tell them I got too hungry to . . . It was hard to eat, and I actually got into the habit of – I would go to blow my nose, and I would keep food in my mouth and then spit it out into a Kleenex and throw it away later.

Then the weight loss started slowing down and I felt frustrated. I felt like I was failing if I couldn't lose a pound a day or whatever. Losing weight made me feel like I'd finally been successful at something; I had pretty low self-esteem. I didn't think I was good at anything. I'm not a good athlete, and where I come from athletics is very, very

was rough – the kids would always call us, like, twins and stuff like that, and I didn't really like that, because we look a lot alike. I think she was a little bit thinner than me.

After I started losing weight, my mom made me get on the scale. I think I was down to 120 when my mom noticed. But I just kept denying everything, and they couldn't really do anything about it since they didn't have any real proof of what I was doing. But a couple of months later – I think when I was just about 100 – the school counselor phoned them. So then my parents thought, well, the obvious thing to do is just to make me eat. So they'd be up at breakfast, trying to get me to eat, trying to force me. But then they saw that didn't work either. I'd just say, "I'm not eating. You can't make me eat." There was a lot of tension in the house. I think once my sister just kind of laid into me, letting me know what I was doing to everyone else in the house, making them unhappy and worried.

Then my parents started making me go to a doctor in Winnipeg

goal weight for me: I was 98 when I went in and they wanted me at 105. So I basically just said, "Well, I'll eat it, I'll get out, and I'll lose the weight again." And I would get visits from the psychiatrist there, but his visits were just basically, "I'm just stopping by to say hi, and I'll come back and see you in a few days." I'm not sure why he saw me, it was totally pointless.

I just felt very isolated and alone. No one could understand. Everyone outside it thought it was just a simple thing of eating, but they didn't understand that I couldn't do that anymore. They just couldn't understand that I couldn't stop myself from wanting to lose weight just because they told me to, and it had kind of become deeper than that.

When I got out of the hospital I went to another psychiatrist. I went to him once and I ended up pretty much in tears when I left because he was pretty cruel. He actually told me, "Oh, you're not too thin." He knew nothing about eating disorders. He basically told

ABOVE, LEFT TO RIGHT: WITH HER SISTER STACEY AT AGE TWO; WITH HER MOM AT SIX MONTHS; AT 11 MONTHS. OPPOSITE PAGE: WITH HER CAT AT AGE 17.

me that I was afraid of becoming a woman. So I went back to the psychiatrist I had seen prior to going into the hospital, and he was pretty good. The only trouble was that he worked at the mental hospital, so I was afraid of getting put in there – and I wouldn't talk to him, pretty much. I wouldn't open up to him at all. I thought I was fat, and I was

convinced everyone was just out to get me.

I was still losing weight. My parents had gotten to the point where they really didn't force me to eat anymore. My doctor's approach was basically, "Eat or go to the hospital." The psychiatrist was leaving the hospital decision pretty much up to the doctor. When I got down to 96 pounds she wanted to put me in the mental hospital. I just refused. There was no way I was going there. And my parents didn't really want me to go to that place, because we'd had a tour through it, and my mom knew I could not survive in a place like that.

Once I got to 94 pounds I struck a deal with my psychiatrist that I would eat a little bit more and try to maintain my weight. He was willing to accept that. But then I started getting worried about getting weighed in gym again, because I was going to tenth grade. So I just started losing. My parents decided I'd better go see a doctor, just to keep tabs on everything. This doctor weighed me and saw that I was in the 80s. So I switched doctors again – this one didn't threaten me with the hospital at all. His goal was basically to have me see that there was a problem, because I didn't see that I was anorexic yet. When I first started seeing him I was in the low 80s, and over the next couple of months I dropped down into the 70s.

Fighting a long, lonely battle for acceptance, self-worth

by Sylvia Kaposi
Staff Writer

Heather Todd could probably be described as one of the lucky ones.

Entering Carman Memorial Hospital in February of 1994 weighing just over 60 pounds, Heather used the incredible self-determination that caused

This Hunger

A four-part series exploring one family's struggle with

"If I can somehow stop even one person from ending up like me, then it will be worth it," she comments.

Heather has addressed students from grades three through 11, and has also talked with teachers to help them identify ways they can help students struggling with eating disorders.

in October of 1994. A year later, she stands by the definition of recovery, but still doesn't see herself making much progress.

She still weighs herself, she still counts calories. She thinks about food a lot - not obsessively, but a lot, nevertheless. She is frustrated by not being able to break out of the diet mentality. She wants to get past this 'stuck' stage but

I STARTED WRITING IN A JOURNAL WHEN I WAS 12. I HAVE ALWAYS USED IT AS A WAY OF RECORDING THE HAPPIEST, SADDEST, AND MOST EXCITING EVENTS THAT HAVE TAKEN PLACE, AND AS A WAY OF VENTING MY FEELINGS AND THOUGHTS. AT THE AGE OF 14 I DEVELOPED AN EATING DISORDER AND I BEGAN TO WRITE IN MY JOURNAL EVEN MORE. THERE HAVE BEEN A LOT OF DIFFERENT EMOTIONS THAT I HAVE HAD WITH THE EATING DISORDER, MOST OF THEM NEGATIVE, AND I HAVE FOUND KEEPING A JOURNAL A GOOD WAY TO ORGANIZE MY THOUGHTS AND GET OUT ALL THE BAD FEELINGS INSTEAD OF HAVING THEM EAT ME UP INSIDE. I HAVE NEVER SET A DEFINITE SCHEDULE OF WHEN I HAVE TO WRITE. I DON'T EVEN WRITE EVERY DAY. I JUST DO IT WHENEVER THE MOOD TAKES ME. THE ONLY TIMES THAT I WILL ALMOST ALWAYS WRITE IS AFTER APPOINTMENTS WITH MY DOCTOR OR MY PSYCHOLOGIST AND AFTER ATTENDING THE EATING DISORDER SUPPORT GROUP. THIS WAY I CAN KEEP TRACK OF WHAT WE DISCUSSED INSTEAD OF JUST PUSHING IT TO THE BACK OF MY MIND. THERE MAY HAVE BEEN A REALLY GOOD IDEA OR SUGGESTION THAT I WASN'T READY TO USE AT THE TIME AND FORGOT ABOUT. THEN IF I READ BACK AT ANOTHER TIME I MAY DECIDE TO USE IT. WHEN I READ BACK IN MY JOURNAL I FIND IT A GOOD WAY OF SEEING WHETHER OR NOT I AM MAKING PROGRESS IN RECOVERY WITH THE EATING DISORDER. THE ONLY NEGATIVE THING I HAVE FOUND IS THAT I WILL AT TIMES WRITE NEGATIVE THINGS ABOUT MYSELF OR SEE THAT I AM NOT MAKING ANY PROGRESS IN RECOVERY AND I THEN TEND TO FEEL WORSE ABOUT MYSELF. OVERALL, THOUGH, I HAVE FOUND WRITING IN A JOURNAL A VERY POSITIVE EXPERIENCE AND STRONGLY RECOMMEND IT TO OTHERS.

I was starting to suffer. I was cold all the time, and I didn't have energy, and my cuts that I would get, they wouldn't heal, and I had scabs on the back of my head. I was just getting weaker. Like, I eventually got to the point where I could barely get up the stairs. I was getting chest pains, and there would always be a loud noise in my ears. I couldn't sleep ever. It was getting hard to walk to and from classes – that would make me calories a day I got really upset. I thought I was getting fat – or fatter, actually. I did start to feel a bit better, but I was more concerned with how I looked.

I was in the hospital for five months. I was eating about 1,600 calories a day, and I think I was 80 pounds, and I finally said, "I'm ready to go home, I think." And I had to see my doctor and my psychiatrist weekly and maintain my calorie intake and everything. But it was

feel really tired. I couldn't pick up my cat anymore. A friend of my mom's told her that people didn't even like to look at me. I was sort of starting to see that maybe there was something wrong. At the beginning of February, when I was in tenth grade, I just could not carry on because of the way my health felt. So I said to my mom, "Well, yeah, I'll go in the hospital." My kidneys were starting to show some problems, because I was drinking only three Diet Cokes a day and nothing else. So I had to go on an IV. My doctor and I had decided together that I would start off eating 300 calories a day, and I would increase 50 calories every day. It was pretty hard – soup made me full. And I was just scared – I was so sure I was going to gain weight right away. I weighed myself once a day, and when I got up to 1,000 hard. I had been trying to cut back on weighing myself. Because before I went in the hospital, I would weigh myself 10 to 15 times a day. And it was really hard at first to eat. I didn't like seeing the weight come on. I wanted to stay at 80 pounds. I felt comfortable there.

Now I weigh about 105 and I'm 5'5". I would rather be thinner. I stopped seeing my doctor a year-and-a-half ago, I guess. I was supposed to go back and see him. But it's just impossible with classes – I go to college now. When I'm not in class I go to the gym once a day. I spend 45 minutes on the Stairmaster or just running. I usually try to eat three meals a day, but it's hard, because I feel like I'm eating so much. I still don't have the energy that I used to have, and also cuts and stuff won't heal as fast as what they used to. And headaches and sleep problems. That's about it. I've had different tests done because of heart palpitations, but they've all come across as normal.

I don't really like my looks. I devote a good portion of the day, like three-quarters of it or so, to my appearance. I don't like to leave my room without makeup on. I wear foundation and mascara and eye shadow and eyeliner every day, but not very heavy. Just light colors.

If there was a way I could make my face look not so round . . . I still constantly think about, like, weight and food at least 90 to 95 percent of the time. Some days even 99 percent of the time.

I don't think the ideal is very healthy. I did read a lot of teen magazines or whatever, and I . . . I don't know. In most of those magazines, the ideal was pretty emaciated looking. When I started thinking of what my definition of thin was, that's probably where it came from. You know, I had the opportunity to go to Paris last spring, and it was hard to find diet drinks and stuff. It just seemed like there wasn't the pressure, and there was so much different food and stuff around. I never saw any of the diet products that there are in Canada – every type of food here is "lite" and

diet and fat-free. Most restaurants there didn't even carry Diet Coke. I started thinking, Well, maybe here they don't worry about it as much. But for the most part, it still seemed like there were a lot of thin women around.

I don't know . . . everyone always talks about a person's appearance, not really what's inside of them or whatever. And there's more pressure from society and other girls and stuff to be thin. There's always sort of a competition between them – who can look the best to attract guys or succeed or whatever. So many of the girls at university, they all think that they're too heavy. The guys are wolfing down, like, five hamburgers at midnight or whatever, and the girls are like, "Oh, I can't eat before bed." When you're in your mid- to late teens, it seems like that's what all the girls are wanting to get, the attention of guys.

For me, it's hard. I'm pretty self-conscious, especially around the guys here, because they're all pretty loud and stuff. And I don't have the confidence to just walk into a room and strike up conversation with people and get to know people. I think, Well, if they want me around, they can come ask me. I think that one doctor who said I was afraid of becoming a woman could have been partially right, but it wasn't the whole reason. I do think it's kind of scary for some girls to go through that, and they're kind of confused as to who they are or what's going on with them. I know for sure that's not the whole reason, but it was a contributing factor.

Right now my relationship with food seems to be the one that's there the most. I've pretty much resigned myself to it – I get really sick of it, but I still like to be in control of it. It would probably be a good idea for me to kind of keep in touch with the doctors and stuff. ❀

Hilary Small

18 years old
Born in Missouri,
lives in Kentucky, U.S.A.

HILARY SMALL, ZINE EDITRIX/PHOTOGRAPHER/
FASHION MAVEN, ON HER INFLUENCES:

Living in a Trailer by the Woods

I lived with my mom and dad in a trailer in Missouri until I was four. We were in a town called Wyatt – it was like a speck in the road. There's not even a stoplight there. It was an awful, depressing place – there are horrible vibes there. My parents had no money back then. Next we moved the trailer to Kentucky Lake, over to this place where there were no other houses. My mom had really bad back problems, and the whole time I was little, she was pretty much bedridden. And my dad was gone most of the time, starting up different plants [he owns a propane gas company], so I never saw much of him. For a long time I thought I was the only kid in the world. So I was always in the woods, playing by myself. I built little houses and forts, and I just lived hanging out in the creeks and playing with snakes and frogs and stuff. I had, like, so much going on in the woods.

Catholic School and Punk Rock

Until I was in ninth grade, I was in a private Christian school. I started freaking out really bad. I was really sheltered. The people that I was thrown in with were just, like, stuck in time. They were totally wrapped up in this cultlike religion – in everything else being Satanic and stuff. So I transferred to a Catholic school in a big town called Paducah, in western Kentucky. That was great. There were a lot of cool people at the Catholic school; skateboarders and people that were into punk rock. My older cousin introduced me to punk music, and I started listening to the Descendants and the Sex Pistols. And the Riot Grrrl movement had just started up, and then

How long it takes me to get ready for a party (with details on what's involved):

i'm always ready for a party.

How long it takes me to get ready for school (with details on what's involved): when i was in skool i'd get up 1/2 an hour early just so i could go back to sleep in the shower. then it took me about 2 seconds to grab my coffee and pour myself into my truck.

I found out about indie rock. I read *Sassy* a lot, and my best friend and I got inspired to start a magazine of our own. We called it *Butterknife Junior*, and we wrote about the health food in our town, and we did record reviews, and we had a "What Sucks" column, and we were totally into *Ren & Stimpy* when nobody had heard of it – I mean, where we lived. It was something nobody in the school had ever seen, and here we were, these two freshman girls, putting this stuff out. All the senior guys just thought we were kick-ass. We were cool.

Kentucky

I just love it. It's full of people that have zero style, but they *do*, in a way. I look at them and just think they're so fantastic. Like, I'll see the most ultimate redneck in a lumber-yard, and he'll be wearing this cheesy agricultural cap and these totally broken-down blue jeans that fit him so good – and if you look at him closely, he looks like a J. Crew model. These people are beautiful, and nobody has noticed it.

Bullies

I've had problems with people my whole life because I'm skinny. When I was in kindergarten, there was this fat girl who would try to strangle me every day. She'd pick me up by my neck. I still see her every once in a while – now she acts like it never happened. And one time I was on the school bus when I was little, and these two fat girls made me sit in between them, like they were going to beat me up, and they took my Pac-Man folder and they ripped it in half because I was skinny and they were fat. I used to get called "Tweetie Bird" and "Shrimp" and all sorts of skinny-girl names when I was little. I was always teased about my weight, and it's going to haunt me for the rest of my life. ▽

Kate Moss

When that waif thing happened, man, I was so happy! Because that was *me*. I'm a waif, and I've always been one, and I was so happy that it was finally, like, cool.

OPPOSITE PAGE: FASHION SKETCH BY HILARY. INSET: AN ISSUE OF HER ZINE, *BUTTERKNIFE JUNIOR*.

My deep dark beauty secrets: i hopelessly buy clothes on impulse. i'll buy something just to watch it hang in my closet.
i will live and die wearing a white spaghetti strapped tanktop. it's my second skin.

When I felt the most/least beautiful: i feel most beautiful fresh from the shower with a white towel on my head. i feel most beautiful when i'm alone in the woods or floating in the ocean. i feel most beautiful when i'm driving my truck. i feel most beautiful when i'm strung out and dirty. i feel ugly when i'm cold or PALE.

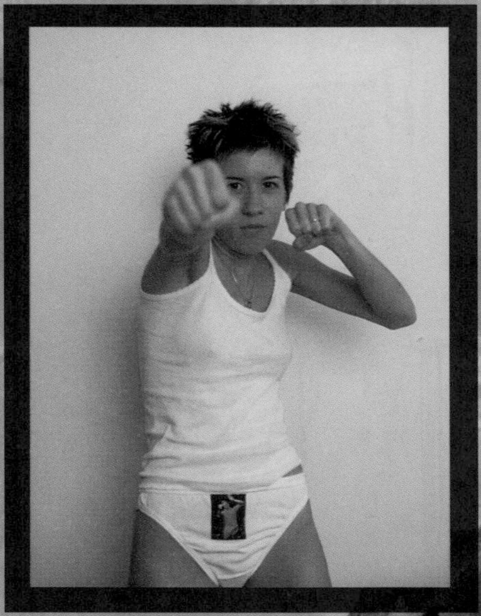

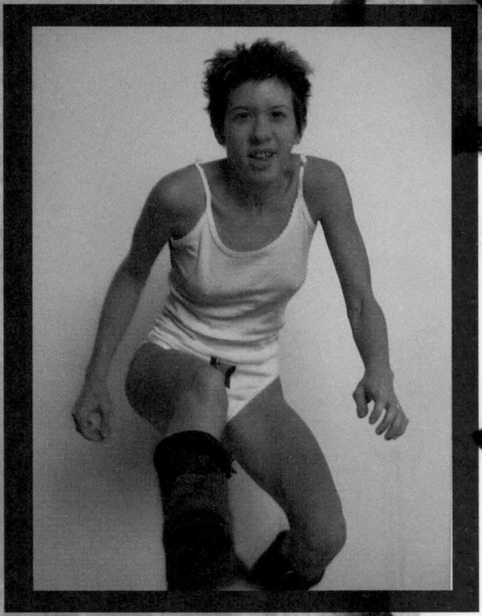

I freak out if I leave home without my: contact drops, a popsicle, and my tuff leather arm band that Jutta Neuman made me to wear around my bicep, so i'll know just how buff i'm getting. i really just got it to make me look cool when i was glassblowing, but now it never comes off.

refuses

to

lie

down

butterknife

junior

issue #bumpkin

neubane

And people were *so* down on it, I couldn't believe it. I just wanted to scream at all these people who were writing letters to the magazines saying how horrible Kate Moss looked. Because I have always looked like this. I have always been thin, and I don't have an eating disorder. I'm really tiny. I'm about 5'7" and my normal weight is 100 pounds. I've tried so hard to gain weight, and it just doesn't happen. I still have this skinny-girl-leg complex – I refuse to wear shorts, and I still get paranoid every time I put on a skirt.

The Lower East Side, New York City

I moved to New York when I was 17 because I met a wonderful-wonderful-wonderful guy. He was 28, and all his friends were in indie rock bands, and made films and they all knew each other. Everybody's an artist, or going on tour or something creative and fantastic. Much different than the frat boys back home. I learned a lot from them – they're all amazing. It was really cool, coming from a place like Kentucky, and then going to New York and being with these people who, you know, walk down the street and people will notice them because they know who they are. It's just a really cool feeling. And I liked walking around the streets in the East Village and knowing the people who were inside the stores, who owned the stores, who were just hanging out.

think I was that ugly, but I was so much a tomboy that I wasn't accepted as a girl. It was totally confusing. But eventually I figured it all out. I figured out how to be tough and feminine at the same time, how to blend it and make it work to my advantage. Then boys started to notice me, and I felt like people thought I was

pretty for once. And when I started going out with guys, and they would give me compliments on whatever different part of my body they thought was attractive, I totally filed it away. I also figured out that boys are really dumb, and I started to use this to my advantage.

Boys

I was so convinced I was a boy until, God, like I was 14. And then I kind of realized I was a girl, and I *hated* it. I cried because I hated the way I looked so much. I hated my face. I didn't want to have breasts. I hated, like, *being a girl*. The girls I grew up with were stupid. They were always crying and whining, and just being so pathetic. And I was so into being tough. Like, all my friends who were girls when I was in elementary school were going out with all my friends who were guys, and I was just one of the guys, and I didn't understand it. I didn't really

Jenny of Label

One day this friend of mine and I went down to Label in New York City to check out various stuff. And this girl Jenny was totally into what I was wearing. I had on these old man's golf pants, like green-and-blue plaid, and then I'm in this skinny strapped tank top and a leather cowboy hat. She asked me if I would do some

Top: Fashion sketch by Hilary.
Center: Self-portrait with bison, 1995.

Who has taught me about beauty:
Nan Goldin. J. Morgan Puett. Juliana Hatfield's "hey babe."
trailer parks and white trash. cowboys and high rollers.
and living in the east village.

58

Things I inherited that I wish I hadn't ~~blah blah~~:
i got the saggy eyelids. got them from mom and her mom. one day they'll be halfway down to my ankles and i'll have to cut them off. tragic situation.

modeling for them, so I did. She's one of the most amazing people I've ever met. She's 30, although she doesn't seem like it at all. She is just super intensely creative and so smart.

White

I've been spending some time in Florida, and I don't have to wear a lot of clothes there. I feel like showing my skin and my face is just as important as wearing clothes. And sometimes I want to put more emphasis on my skin or hair, so I'll wear a lot of white. I never wear makeup. I'll wear powder. I've just never done it, and I don't feel like I need it. Every once in a while, I'll think, I have to do something to my eyes. I have kind of long eyelashes, so I don't really need to wear mascara. I'm just taking advantage of it, that I don't have to wear makeup. Someday I'll probably have to. I just don't want to till then.

Steven Alan

He owns a store on Wooster Street in New York City, and he's a massive influence on me. He carries every great, young downtown designer in New York right now and sends me care packages full of clothes by Rebecca Dannenberg, Built by Wendy, Daryl K. I really love Rebecca's skirts – they're, like, knee-length and straight. I almost always wear a spaghetti strap top with one of those. And Daryl's pants really fit me well – they're supersmall. Other pants are too baggy for me – I don't have thighs. All those designers make stuff that

The best beauty tricks I've learned (about applying mascara, eyeliner, lipstick, etc.):
my number one rule is to never never look like my 9th grade english teacher.

they would want to wear for themselves. That's what I want to do. I can see an article of clothing and I can deconstruct it and build it back to how I want it. That's what I want to do, because I can never find a thing that fits me.

White Trash

I try to always get an element of white trash in whatever I wear. It's hard to explain it, maybe it's just an attitude. I'm into leather stuff, like cowboy-biker stuff. You know the whole thing that happened this past year with the ugliness? There was a white-trash flavor to everything. I was thrilled when that happened, because it meant that I might have a chance at doing this stuff. Because I'm not conventionally pretty or anything. I have a pretty bizarre style. I have a face that people would recognize. It's not just, like, a blend-in blond kind of face. And I would show my mom pictures – in *I-D* magazine or something, in some crazy editorial, and she'd just be like, "You know, this is so ugly! These people don't even look like models!" And I was like, "Mom, don't you understand? These people, who aren't really pretty by society's standards, are models! They're able to be considered beautiful." ✿

I can't live without my (name products or potions or whatever you like):
everything for my hair (including Raymond and Victoria), Karin Herzog VitaAKombi, origins spot remover, and i'll tell you what, Bliss NYC rocks. i'm a total spa junkie. i'm constantly discovering better products to control and manipulate the wonderous hair and skin.
Bumble + Bumble.

My favorite homemade beauty concoction(s) (in recipe form):
1/3 suntan
1/3 vanity
1/3 hanging out the window of a fast car
= one girl with a fiery passion.   a punK.

FASHION SKETCH BY HILARY

Opposite page and this page, clockwise from top left: By CB; today, by Charity; by Alanna Gabin; at 18 months; by CB; by CB; self-portrait in bathroom; feeding her dog Twiglet in 1996, by Alanna Gabin; pink roadside barn photographed by Hilary; the rest are by CB.

AT JUST 13, IZMIRA Tawfeek is the most promising ballerina at the school of New York's Dance Theatre of Harlem, where she's on full scholarship. She began dancing, she tells me, when she was three years old. "My mother put me in dancing because she said I was hyper," says Izmira, who adds that she was never really all that into dance. "And, basically, she wanted to keep me off the streets."

Izmira lives with her mother in an apartment in Harlem, in New York City. During the week, she gets up at around 6:30 or 7:00, washes up, gets dressed, and eats breakfast. "I'll eat anything that's there," she says proudly. Then she gets on the subway and goes to school on 77th Street. When school's over, she gets back on the subway and takes it all the way up to 148th Street, then walks nine blocks to the dance school. She has a half hour to change and eat something before heading into class, which can last till 6:30 or 7:00. "Then I go home, eat dinner, wash up, and go to bed," she says. "That's it." On Saturdays, she helps teach younger girls at the Dance Theatre, which she likes a lot. "Ballet is beautiful," she tells me, "but it's a lot of hard work. It's hard, very hard." When I ask her what's the hardest part, Izmira says it's keeping her balance. "It's difficult, holding everything together so that you can stay in one place," she says. "And making your leg go really high is hard, too." But Izmira knows that as trying as certain moves may be, the way she's built makes it easier for her than some other dancers. "I like to show off a little," she admits, "but not too much." What qualifies as too much? "It's like, if everybody has to be a certain height, then you go

higher," she explains. "Or if you have a certain step, not to go overboard with it. Because that makes the other dancers look bad."

Things that Izmira loves about ballet:

1. The discipline. "We're not supposed to talk," she says. "When it comes to dancing, I keep discipline. Because if the music is playing and people are talking, it will get too noisy, and you can't hear what the teacher is saying. You can keep your concentration when you're not talking."

2. The health benefits. "It keeps me really fit and it keeps me thin," says Izmira. "I know if I didn't dance, I'd probably be chubby by now, because I love to eat everything. If the food is good, I want to eat it." Izmira knows that it's unusual for a dancer not to be flipped out about being super super skinny, and says she unfortunately knows plenty of other dancers who are.

These are the things about ballet that Izmira is less than psyched about:

1. Time. "Sometimes, it's like, 'I don't want to go to dance; I want to go to such-and-such a place with my friend,' or 'I want to do something else, like have fun, instead of going to class every single day.' It gets to be boring most of the time. There's no time for anything else."

2. The physical suffering. "The first time I went on to toe shoes, I was like, 'Oh, I can do this – this

Izmira Tawfeek
Dance Student
13 years old
Born and lives in New York, U.S.A.

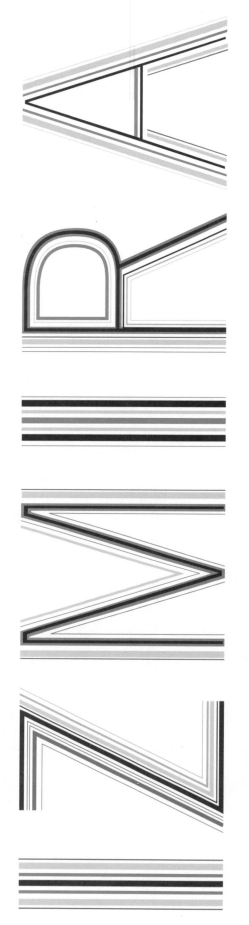

How long it takes me to get ready for school: About an hour and 15 minutes, because I spend so much time in the bathroom getting dressed, eating, and fixing my hair, so that I can look decent in public.

MY DEEP, DARK BEAUTY SECRET: DRINK A LOT OF WATER.

Top to bottom: Age eight; age four; one year.

CB

CB

Age 12

CB

WHO HAS TAUGHT ME ABOUT BEAUTY: MY MOTHER HAS TAUGHT ME ALL ABOUT BEAUTY, AS MUCH AS SHE KNOWS.

I feel the most beautiful when: I go shopping. I like to experiment with different looks to see what really looks good on me.

I WASH MY HAIR: ONCE A WEEK WITH I.C. SHAMPOO, BECAUSE IT KEEPS MY BRAIDS SHINY AND SUPPLE.

I freak out if I leave home without my: Earrings and something to put on my mouth like Chapstick or lipstick.

Something I inherited I wish I hadn't/things I inherited and love: I wish I hadn't inherited my hair from my mother. I have always wanted long hair. I love the eyes that I inherited, but they could be a touch lighter.

looks easy.' Then, when I started, it was, like, pain. And in pointe class, my feet just hurt. It's weird! If it looks so easy, you think it shouldn't hurt. But it does."

One of the coolest things about the Dance Theatre of Harlem is that the school has a strict policy regarding the leotards, tights, and slippers: Everything must be dyed to match the individual skin tone of the dancer, so most of the costumes are dark brown instead of the typical pink, which tends to flatter white skin. Izmira loves this rule, and I think it's amazing, too. The founder and artistic director of the school, Arthur Mitchell, told me that he instituted this rule because so many of the students are of different ethnic backgrounds. "When you see one shade of skin tone at the top of the body, you should see the same below," he says. "You should not break the line."

Izmira tells me that the Dance Theatre, and ballet in particular, have given her a sense of pride and accomplishment, and that she feels happiest about her appearance when she's performing. Dance makes up for those days, she tells me, when she looks in the mirror and is plagued by a general sense of dissatisfaction with her face. Because while she's not anorexic or obsessed with perceived imperfections in her body, her face is another story. "Usually I think my face is fine," she says. "But I don't like my teeth – I don't like my gap. I want them to be closed, like the perfect teeth." Still, she says that performing makes her feel unequivocally beautiful. "It's because, when you dance, it's like expressing yourself the best way you can," she says. "And you're showing everybody, 'This is me! This is how I dance. Look at me! Look at how I feel!'" ✦

AGE EIGHT

Kirsten Dunst

Actress
14 years old
Born in New Jersey,
lives in California, U.S.A.

WHAT I LOVE RIGHT NOW

Brad Pitt (First on-screen kiss, *Interview with the Vampire*)

Brad was like a hang-loose guy. We would do the stupidest things. I remember this one time, we took a bunch of junk in his dressing room, ketchup and mustard, and flushed it down the toilet. It was so funny. We took a picture of it. But Tom Cruise was more of a father-type figure, 'cause he has kids and stuff. So he wasn't as goofy as Brad.

Shopping

I usually go to Rampage and Wet Seal and Contempo Casuals – that store's really cheap. I also go to Melrose sometimes. I love Fred Segal's, that's one of my favorite stores. But he's just so expensive. One of my graduation presents was from there. I got these really cool blue satin pants and a shirt to match. And they have cool stuff at the Gap now. They usually have boring stuff, but I think they're trying to get trendy or whatever. Oh, you know what I want so bad? I love Donna Karan. My friends are like, "Who is that?" They have the most expensive stuff, it's not even funny. But, oh, there's this silvery dress that ties up below your neck, and it's got spaghetti straps. It's so pretty and it flows out. Then there's this Versace dress I love so much. Oh my God, it's the most beautiful dress I've ever seen in my life. It's red on the top, and then it's light blue, and then when it gets to the bottom, it's red again. Oh, I love it so much. I obviously love expensive dresses. I wanted it for homecoming, and my mom was like, "What!?"

Cheerleading

That was a lot of fun, just being with my friends. It makes you feel like you're a part of the school more. I didn't try out for my high school [squad] this year, though. They're really strict about it, so if I'm gone for a certain amount of games or something, they'd probably kick me off the team anyway.

Feng Shui

It's this thing where you organize your house or your bedroom in a certain way – like, if you want peace, you're not supposed to have any corners in your room. So I might do that, or I might do a psychic-y theme – like, I want to have stars and the moon and stuff like that in my room.

Tattoos

I want to get one on my ankle. I want a ladybug for good luck, or a little flower, or a fairy, or an angel that will protect me or something like that. My mom says when I'm older I can get it. She even wants one, too, an angel on her ankle. Wow!

Catholic School Uniform

I have a blue skirt, and white-and-navy-blue polo shirts, the regular socks, and my Doc Martens. They say, "You know, your skirts shouldn't be more than a couple of inches above your knees," but everyone's is, like, so short. It saves the hassle every morning of getting up and thinking about what you're going to wear.

Pilatés

It's an exercise that dancers do when they're not dancing. You work out with all this special equipment, and it doesn't bulk you up so you have bulky *✗* muscles. It gives you more of an elongated look, and it makes your muscle tone nicer and your posture straighter. It's really fun, so I do that sometimes. Actually, I never have time to do it.

George Clooney

I'm doing a couple of *ER* episodes. I'm playing, like, a street-kid hooker, and George starts to take care of me. He's so nice. But I never get crushes. Why would I get a crush? He's, like, 30-something. He's old! Actually, he might even be, like, 40.

Makeup

I like MAC a lot, so I have my MAC rouge, I have my Prescriptives powder, and then I have my creamy cover-up, and then I have mascara, and then I put on eye shadow. You know that area right below your eyebrow? If you put a little bit of white under there – a tone lighter than your color skin – it opens your face up. Your whole face looks so pretty if you put, like, a little bit on your eyebrows. And I knew this one girl who got, like, brushes, and used the brush on her mascara, and then put it on her eyes so it wasn't all clumpy or anything like that. And it goes on perfect. She just used a brush and brushed it against the mascara, and put it on my eyelashes. And it looked so much prettier than using the little stick-on things.

Cats and Dogs 🐕

Oh, I love cats. We have four little kitties – they're like a half-year old – and then we have, like, my old cat, and she's, like, 17! And then we inherited this dog because the person who had it before said, "You know, he likes it better with you. Why don't you just take care of him?" It works, 'cause we have a pretty big house.

WHAT I CAN'T STAND

Hippie Chicks

It's so annoying. It's like, "That was a couple of years ago, dears." I don't know. I was kind of into it, too, but like, "Peace, Love, and Happiness" and all that hippie junk – ugh, I couldn't stand it. Are you trapped in, like, your mother's time period now?

Alanis Morissette

She's starting to get annoying. Obviously she had a really bad time with her boyfriend . . . I don't know. I liked her music, but now it's getting like she needs new stuff. I'm getting kind of sick of her.

Complexion

I'm not happy because I'm so . . . I'm not white, pale like a ghost, but I have a really light complexion and everything. And I have such dark circles under my eyes which I inherited from my mom, so I always have to use cover-up. I wish I were a little bit more tan, because like all these girls are tan, and I want to be tan. But I can't tan. I burn.

Popular Girls

There isn't actually the, like, popular group in this school that

HOW LONG IT TAKES ME TO GET READY FOR A PARTY: AN HOUR AND A HALF. IT DEPENDS ON WHO IS GOING TO BE THERE, IF I WANT TO DO MY HAIR CURLY, OR IF I WANT TO DO ANY EXTRA-SPECIAL JOB ON MAKEUP.

WHO HAS TAUGHT ME ABOUT BEAUTY: MY MOM AND MAGAZINES.

I'm going to now, but there was in the other school I went to. They were a bunch of bitches.

Smile

I hate that I have a dimple. I can't stand it! My friend keeps telling me, "That means you have excess fat on your face." And when I smile, it goes crooked on one of the sides. You know how Alicia Silverstone smiles, how it goes crooked on one side? That's what

lisp when I talk. They're a pain in the butt.

Buying by Mail

I just ordered a bunch of clothes and I'm returning three things. Some of the stuff, the way it looks in the catalogue is nothing like how it looks when you get it. I ordered this shirt from Dollhouse, and it has a little snowflake on it and it's light blue with, like, dark blue trim. But it's so ugly! And it's

big in areas where it shouldn't be and stuff like that. And I'm returning these tank tops that aren't sewn together properly. It's really weird. They can't, like, sew tank tops together? That's probably why they were so cheap.

The Lack of Cute Boys

I don't like anyone in school. I'm so bummed. Because it's more fun when you go to school and you're like, "Oh yeah, I like him,"

happens with mine. I don't like that. I just want a straight, normal smile. And I have these removable braces, except they don't look like braces. They look like a funny-looking retainer. So I have to wear those, but I never wear them at school, because I'm talking to my friends, and they're like, "Take that thing out! I can't understand you!" I'd wear them, but they make me have a

you know? I don't like anyone. So I just go to school, do my schoolwork, don't have any guys to look at because I don't like any of them. My mom won't let me date till I'm 15, but still . . .

Styling Tips in Magazines

It's so funny, because I saw this one hairdo I really liked, and I tried to do it on my hair, but it just didn't work. It was really cute – the

bangs were done over to one side, and she had all these parts in, like, the perfect spots and everything. And I went, "Okay, 🐟 let me try this in my hair." But it's like all the things in magazines; it never works on your hair.

Disrespecting the Ladies

Too-Short – he has the worst songs. I bought his CD because I liked this one song, "Gettin' It." And oh my God! It was so disgusting. It's just disgusting what they say about women! I'm just like, "What's your problem? You think that bashing women is, like, great?" Mom was so mad at me. She was like, "What the hell are you listening to?"

🐟 Hair

I wish I had shorter hair. I've had long hair all my life. I'm just getting sick of it. I'm like, "Mom, I want to cut my hair!" And she says, "Oh no, you have beautiful hair! Keep it!" She always tries to make me feel better about myself. I guess it's hard to think of the stuff you like about yourself. 🐟

The best beauty tricks I've learned: For mascara: Put the mascara on an eye shadow brush and use that to apply the mascara. For eyeliner: Put a shade lighter than your skin on your eyebrow bone to open up your eyes and face.

THINGS I INHERITED AND LOVE: MY DOG "BEAUTY."

When I feel the most beautiful: After I visit José Eber.

I FREAK OUT IF I LEAVE HOME WITHOUT MY: CLOTHES ON.

CB

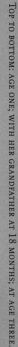

HOW LONG IT TAKES ME TO GET READY FOR SCHOOL: A HALF HOUR FOR MAKEUP AND HAIR. I HAVE A UNIFORM FOR SCHOOL SO I DON'T NEED TO WORRY ABOUT A WARDROBE. I DON'T NEED TO TAKE A SHOWER BECAUSE I ALWAYS TAKE A SHOWER THE NIGHT BEFORE.

I CAN'T LIVE WITHOUT MY: CLINIQUE CONCEALER, MAC LIPSTICK, PRESCRIPTIVES POWDER.

When I feel the least beautiful: In the morning.

KIRSTEN AT AGE EIGHT WITH HER BROTHER

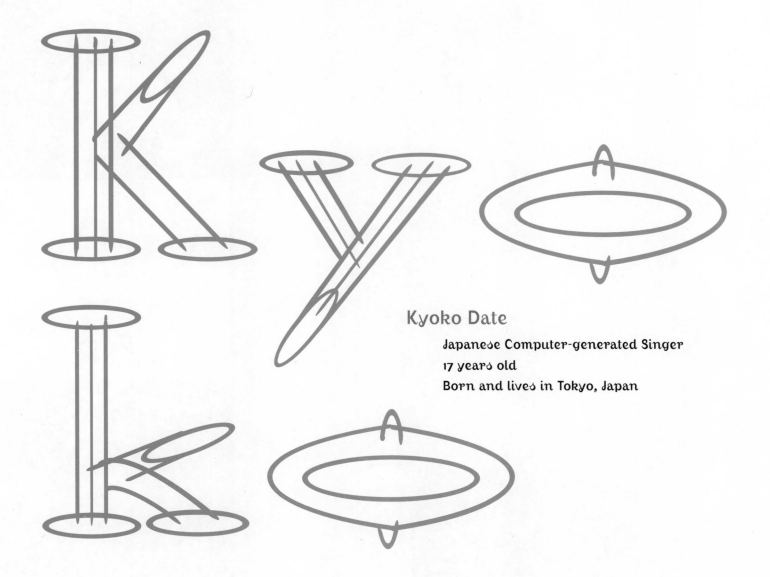

Kyoko Date

Japanese Computer-generated Singer
17 years old
Born and lives in Tokyo, Japan

KYOKO DATE IS A COMPUTER-GENERATED 17-YEAR-OLD WHO WAS BORN AND LIVES IN A SUBURB OUTSIDE TOKYO, JAPAN. IN 1996 SHE RELEASED A SONG CALLED "LOVE COMMUNICATION" AND HOSTS A LIVE RADIO SHOW ONCE A WEEK CALLED "KYOKO DATE DK-96'S G1 GROUPER." HER FAVORITE COLORS ARE BLACK AND WHITE. HER FAVORITE MOVIE IS *TOY STORY*. HER FAVORITE ACTORS ARE CHRISTIAN SLATER AND KYOZO NAGATSUKA. AND HER FAVORITE BODY PART IS "MY WAIST (JOKE)." ARMED WITH THIS INFORMATION, I GOT A CHANCE TO ASK KYOKO SOME QUESTIONS ABOUT HER TAKE ON BEAUTY.

DO YOU EVEN THINK ABOUT ISSUES OF BEAUTY? *I don't want to gain weight, but since I'm still young, I'm not too worried about it.*

YOU HAVE BEEN CALLED A PEER ROLE MODEL. WHAT IMAGE DO YOU WISH TO PORTRAY TO THOSE WHO LOOK UP TO YOU? *I'm not necessarily successful yet. I want to be referred to as a cool girl.*

DO YOU REMEMBER THE FIRST TIME YOU THOUGHT YOU WERE PRETTY OR NOT? *I don't think I'm pretty. I think I'm ugly when I look at the promotion video for my first song. My smile was really unnatural.*

WHAT ROLE DOES BEAUTY PLAY IN YOUR LIFE, AND ARE YOU COMFORTABLE WITH IT? *I'm not satisfied with the way I look now because I want to be prettier and sexier, and I want to look more mature. Since I'm only 17, I guess it's natural to want these qualities.*

I CAN'T LIVE WITHOUT MY: NOTHING REALLY IMPORTANT, BUT I GUESS MY LIP GLOSS.

Something I inherited: I wish I hadn't. I wish I had a smaller mouth.

VIDEO FRAMES ON BOTH PAGES ARE FROM KYOKO'S FIRST MUSIC VIDEO, "LOVE COMMUNICATION."
COURTESY HORIPRO, INC.

ARE THERE WOMEN PAST OR PRESENT YOU CONSIDER TO BE PARTICULARLY
BEAUTIFUL? *I like Mariah Carey, not because her face is pretty but because she
seems to have a nice personality.*

DO YOU FEEL PRESSURE TO CONFORM TO TRADITIONAL NOTIONS OF BEAUTY?
HOW DO YOU FEEL YOU FIT THEM OR DON'T FIT THEM? *I have nothing to
do with "tradition" because I'm a computer graphic human being. So I don't feel
pressured, but I may be a traditional Japanese girl in the sense that I want to
become a happy girl. I like my eyes and hate my ears.*

WHAT'S THE FIRST BEAUTY PRODUCT YOU REMEMBER CHOOSING?
Nivea Skin Cream and Johnson & Johnson Baby Oil.

WHEN DID YOU FIRST START TO THINK SERIOUSLY ABOUT YOUR
APPEARANCE? *When I was in ninth grade.*

WHAT ABOUT TATTOOS? PIERCINGS? *I personally hate tattoos but love
pierced ears!*

DO YOU FOLLOW PARTICULAR FITNESS REGIMENS TO MAINTAIN
YOUR PHYSICAL APPEARANCE? *I'm not on a diet, but I do practice ☜boxing
to stay in shape.*

WHAT ARE YOUR SKIN CARE CONCERNS? *To get enough sleep.*

WHAT DO YOU LOOK LIKE WHEN YOU'RE NOT IN THE SPOTLIGHT?
I probably look spaced out. 🎥

WHAT DO YOU USE TO GET RID OF PIMPLES? *I never get pimples.*

HOW DO YOU PREFER TO WEAR YOUR HAIR? *If I were to have long hair, it would
take up too much memory on the computer, so I have to keep my hair short.*

That's my story. 🌐

WHAT'S IN MY MEDICINE CABINET: I HARDLY GET SICK,
SO ALL I HAVE IS MEDICINE FOR COLDS AND THAT'S ABOUT IT.

How long it takes me to get ready for a party: I don't
go to parties that often, so I have no idea.

The best beauty tricks I've learned: I don't wear much makeup.
Usually only foundation and that's it. I think the best tip is to live an
interesting and exciting life.

Who has taught me about beauty: My mother and friends.

MY DEEP, DARK BEAUTY SECRETS: EAT WELL,
SLEEP WELL, AND MOVE MY BODY A LOT.

SOMETHING I INHERITED AND LOVE: I'M GLAD I INHERITED MY PARENTS' LONG LEGS.

I freak out if I leave home without my: Beeper.

CHRISTAN BURRAN BY VIV

I've known Christan Burran for years. She did my makeup every day — actually, a couple of times a day — for my Lifetime talk show and she's done my makeup for tons of TV appearances and events since then. Whenever we see each other, she's always got some good new beauty tip she discovered. But what I love about her advice is that it's never the same stuff you've heard over and over again in magazines, books, whatever. And what I mostly love about Christan is that she's not into transforming you into something you're not, and she always keeps makeup in its proper place — something to have fun with, not to be a slave to.—JP

Skin Care

Skin care is more important than makeup. If you have problem skin and just cover it up instead of dealing with it, you could exacerbate adult acne or even end up with scarring. It's best to take care of your skin when you are young so that you won't have problems later in life.

Important Things to Remember

Try to avoid soap for washing your face. Instead try foaming cleansers in a light formula. I love Aubrey, which is totally organic, inexpensive, and easy to get at health food stores. Clarins Foaming Cleanser is more expensive at around $15, but it lasts a long time.

Stay away from cream cleansers like Pond's. They are too oily.

Natural skin care products are really the best. Stay away from some popular products that have lots of chemicals, like those from Clinique. If you can spend a little more money, Aveda, and Ling, a small Japanese skin care salon in Soho with a mail order business, are worth saving for.

Exfoliation is super important to remove dead skin cells and impurities — Apricot Scrub or an all-natural scrub like an oatmeal scrub works really well and can be found anywhere for very little. Stay away from the Buff Puff, as it is way too rough.

Never use a scrub more than once a week; it's too abrasive.

Tips

By Christan Burran

I believe in estheticians, who are licensed skin care and makeup specialists (they give you facials), more than dermatologists. Estheticians take care of the problem by cleaning the skin and extracting the bacteria. Dermatologists prescribe medication to clear up the skin, which sometimes works but puts unwanted medicine, like antibiotics, in the body, and can cause undesirable side effects such as overdrying the skin, and dry mouth, or worse.

Most treatments can be done at home – the cleansing, toning, and exfoliation.

In addition, use natural clay masks once a week, twice at most. They really pull out toxins; oil, and impurities. Natural kaolin clay works best and most clay masks are very inexpensive. Queen Helene ("the Cocktail Facial") is available everywhere and it's cheap – around $4.

Try really hard not to pick at your face. This exposes it to bacteria from your fingers, which makes the pimples much worse and can lead to scarring. If you have a lot of pimples, make an appointment with an esthetician. They can extract the pimples, they are cheaper than dermatologists, and you won't have to buy medicine.

The right nutrition and exercise help the skin stay healthy. Remember to drink lots of water. Supplement your meals with as many fruits and vegetables (foods with moisture like most greens are especially good) as you can. Avoid sugar and fried foods. Alcohol and smoking are not only bad for your health but also seriously dehydrate the skin. Soda is not good either – Cindy Crawford is getting paid to advertise.

Most important – stay away from crazy stress. Meditation, yoga, relaxation and breathing exercises really help.

Stress shows up in break-outs in the cheek area. Break-outs in the chin area are usually the result of hormones acting up. Break-outs on your forehead can be caused by your hair, and hair products that are full of oil (especially conditioners). Substitute detangling rinse for heavy conditioners, to minimize the oiliness.

CHRISTAN AT WORK IN BRITISH COLUMBIA

Foundation

Foundation is totally optional for young skin. When I was 16 I felt I needed foundation because of my acne and pimples (which was not the best approach). If applied correctly, however, foundation can help cover the problem areas. If your skin is good and has a healthy glow, I'd say skip it altogether.

Do's and Don'ts

Use only oil-free formulas.

Stay away from creams or heavy coverage.

Most of the time use warm yellow tones – especially on ethnic skin.

The warmer the color of the foundation (beige or yellow as opposed to cool colors like pink or red) the more natural it will look.

Apply foundation using a well-lighted mirror so that you can really blend it in, and see the color.

It's better to apply foundation with a natural sponge, made slightly damp for lighter coverage, rather than fingers. Max Factor's sponge is best – it's like a sea sponge, with tiny pores.

Never buy foundation without trying on the color. And remember to try it on your face, where you'll wear it (the nose is best), rather than your hand.

Try dewy formulas. They have more moisture, are light, and are thinner in texture. They look modern and give a sheen. MAC Face and Body is not too expensive and is fantastic.

Try foundation with a little sparkle! Max Factor has a few "shimmery" shades and is available everywhere. If you can't find one with sparkle, you can always use a sparkly powder.

Concealer

If you don't need foundation but sometimes have a breakout, concealer is your friend! It's great for the darkness around and under the eye area. Girls with dark hair or skin sometimes have more darkness under the eyes – which can look sexy, but it's up to you.

Tricks for Concealer

Dab onto blemishes with a small brush or a Q-Tip, then blend slightly with the finger or a soft sponge.

Always use warm yellow tones. If the concealer is too light, it will not cover well and the darkness will show through.

Cover Girl's and Max Factor's concealers are liquidy and don't cover well. MAC's is quite thick, and one of the best. Prescriptives is liquidy but somehow covers.

To apply under the eye, always use the fingertip. Warm the concealer with your fingers – your body temperature will soften a solid concealer and make it easier to blend.

Stay away from pink tones, and try the shade before buying.

Powder

Powder is useful for keeping other makeup in place. Also, a little powder really gives a nice glow and natural matteness to the skin.

Do's and Don'ts

Most powders at drugstores come in the less flattering pink tones (Cover Girl, etc). But they do last forever.

Try to use warm tones with a smooth texture, which means they have been milled more. Revlon has some of these now.

MIZUO PECK, BY CHERYL DUNN

Loose powder gives less coverage than pressed powder.

Apply with a powder puff and not a brush. The puff helps set the powder; the brush just moves it around the face.

A velour puff is the best (you can get one at any drugstore) and some can be washed and kept for a while. A dirty puff or makeup sponge can cause major breakouts.

Never share your powder puffs like I did in high school.

Eyes

Brows

I think groomed brows are really important for all ages. They frame the eyes and can make us look happy or sad. It is easy to have nice brows – it just takes a little time.

Brow Tricks

If you have great-shaped brows, just brush them up in the morning with a brow brush or use a brow gel (like Brow Tamer by Max Factor) which is clear and will keep brows in place all day. Or just use clear mascara. Hairspray works too, or hair gel. Apply a little to the brush and sweep upward, setting them in place.

Tweeze brows only if necessary. Stray brows above and below the natural brow line can look messy, and can be cleaned up by using nice sharp tweezers (Tweezer Man are the best – thin, sharp, and slanted), and a well-lighted mirror.

If you have time and money, have your esthetician groom your brows for you.

Avoid waxing. The only way to get a natural shape is by tweezing.

Always keep a slight arch to the brow. It should look natural with the arch just above the pupil of the eye.

Sometimes brows are actually darker than your hair. Concealer is a great way to lighten brows. Apply a little medium tone concealer (the same as you use on the rest of your face) with a small brush, and blend over brow hairs using the brush. It makes for a very modern look. You can also use a light shimmery eye shadow, for a very cool effect.

Don't make brows too thin or keep them too thick. Stay in the middle with clean medium-shaped brows.

Eye Shadows

I love eye shadow and think it's fun to wear. It brightens the whole eye area. Eye shadow can be clean and simple or fun and full of color.

Painting on the Shadow

Always apply with a natural hair brush. The synthetic brushes will not blend. You can tell if the brush is natural by looking at the base of it to see the different colors of the actual hairs. Synthetic brushes are all the same color. MAC has great brushes; you can even get good ones at Drug Emporium or Rickie's. Just make sure they're natural.

If you cannot get a real brush, try Q-Tips with a flat end on them or a little sponge-tip applicator. They blend just fine.

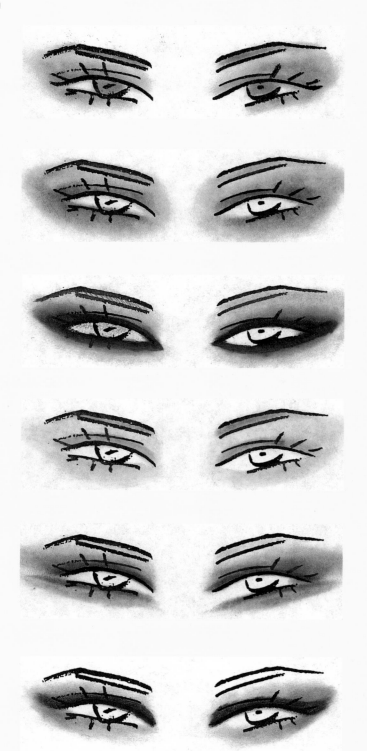

BY NICOLAI GROSELL

Stay with one color over the entire eye. Keep it simple and modern. Try shades like warm beige tones. White shimmery shadow is great. Soft, shiny lilac looks hip. Warm light green is modern. Brown is natural but it's boring. Golds are fun. Drugstores have all these colors but their consistency isn't great. Every once in a while splurge on something from Prescriptives, Chanel, Dior, MAC, or the like.

Creamy eye shadows are great too – you can blend them with your finger. Just a few strokes of color all over the lid and crease up to the brow bone with a light color and you're done. If you can't find one, you can mix moisturizer or Vaseline with powder shadow.

Eye shadow is about choosing the colors you love – there are so many. It doesn't necessarily have to look natural – deep purple or blended black looks great if you're into that, or want to try something different. Try a bright rose or orange tone on the lid and on the lower lash line – it's like a wash of color.

Eyeliner

Eyeliner can be hard to apply and most young girls don't need it. But it is a nice effect and it can open the eye.

Liner Tricks

Too much liner will close the eye, making it look smaller.

For a more natural look, stay with colors like dark gray, brown, black, dark blue, and dark green.

Light-colored eyeliner never really works.

Dark matte eye shadows as liner work great and can be applied with a sponge-tip applicator.

MAC, Chanel, and Lancôme have great black eyeliners. Try liner pens for an even darker look.

Kohl liners sometimes look too heavy and tend to smudge quickly. That's why it's important to get good-quality eyeliner, instead of a cheaper drugstore version.

Focus on the lash line and paint liner there super close. Small, thin, flat brushes work great.

Don't wear too much liner on the lower lashes – it's too heavy and dated.

Eyeliner inside the lower eyelid is hip and was one of my personal favorites when I was 16. Wear it if you like; it gives the eye a mysterious look. Make sure and blend the eyeliner with a sponge-tip applicator into the lower lash line.

Mascara and eyeliner products should not be used for more than a year before being replaced – and that's pushing it.

Curling Your Lashes

Always curl your lashes before applying mascara, otherwise lashes tend to "fall down." Curled lashes always frame the eyes better.

Try the new plastic kind of curlers – they're gentler on the lashes (no breakage) and curl better.

Curler pads should be washed with soap and water every two weeks or so to remove excess/old mascara build-up. (Though remember – you should always try to curl your lashes first before applying mascara.)

Mascara

It is super easy.

Brown is more modern than black and softer on the eye.

Curved brushes work a lot better than straight ones.

Don't wear waterproof mascara unless you need it, because it's too hard to get off.

Find your favorite brand and stick with it, like everyone has already done with Maybelline.

Apply two coats on the upper lashes, always with extra applied to the outer lashes. This creates the most beautiful cat-eye effect.

You can just apply mascara to the upper lashes for a lighter look.

Avoid applying two coats to the lower lashes.

If you're not into a made-up look, just use a clear mascara (Maybelline, Cover Girl, Max Factor all have them).

Blush

I love blush! It brightens the face and balances the eyes and lips.

Blush Tips

Keep it simple but always wear a little.

Try warm shades like bronze or copper. With blush, pinky shades look great too. Tempting Beige by Chanel is the best color ever! MAC has shades that can be used for both eye shadow and blush. They are very versatile.

Don't wear blue-pink or orange blush – it's dated.

Always use your natural hair brush or a cotton puff or soft sponge – it's the only way to blend. Watch out for synthetic cotton balls and pads – only use cotton.

Smile real big and apply to the apples of the cheeks. Then blend a little outward.

Use on temples and forehead for color and balance. Cream blush is easy to apply with a sponge. Blend.

Sometimes if the color is right (a natural, earth tone for instance), you can use the same blush to color the eyelids and cheeks.

Lips

Lips need moisture and a little color. Just find one or two shades you dig and stay with them for a while.

Lip Tips

Never match lipstick to your outfit.

Stay away from super-matte-drying lipsticks, especially dark browns. They look heavy.

Try light formulas like sheers, tones, gloss, moisture-rich formulas, frost, and shimmer. They look modern. The shade is up to you, but I love pearl shades – bronze, lavender, rose, and cherry – for a softer effect.

A beautiful rose-tone gloss is my favorite, or a soft lavender. Kiehl's Golden Berry is great. Think of a lipstick color that looks like your natural color, only brighter or darker, whichever way you want to go. To make lips look darker, use burgundy, wine, or a rose-brown shade. To make them look brighter, use a cherry or a red shade and blend really well.

Try to let some of your natural lip color show through.

If you don't dig lipstick color, wear a lip-treatment product with a little sunscreen like Blistex in the round tube or Kiehl's lip treatment with SPF 15.

Lipliner is good only if you need it to build up thinner lips. But I think liner is somewhat unnatural and unnecessary for young women. If you do use it, be sure to blend it inward well. Try lipliner colors that are natural like Spice & Nutmeg from MAC, or Nude by Chanel, or Nude by Max Factor.

PAULA OSPINA, BY NICOLAI GROSELL

Hair

I love Brad and Chris. These guys have been coloring and cutting my hair since I was a curly-short-dark-haired about-to-be-talk show host. Not that they had to push me to become the long-straight-strawberry-blond that I am now. I've always loved playing around with my hair. From when my friend Jesse and I played beauty parlor (I was five) and she cut my long Laurie Partridge-style to around an inch from my head. Two inches in some chunks. Since then I've been platinum blond, auburn, dark brown, buzzcut, Cleopatra, boyish (during my nose-ring phase), long in the front/short in the back (circa 1981).

And even for those of us who don't mind a little change, it's still a rare and great thing to be able to trust your hair-cutter or colorist enough to sit down in the chair and say "Whatever you think." Because that's how I feel about these guys, I wanted to share them with you. And they agreed. Here are Chris Cusano's hair-cutting and Brad Johns's coloring words of wisdom.—JP

Hair Tips

If you see a great haircut on someone, don't be shy. Ask them where they got it.

If your hair is coarse, dry, or frizzy, there is a wide range of de-frizzing products, gels and sprays, for home use that can cure this instantly. I recommend Brad Johns Hair Tranquilizer, but there are many products out there. You have to ask your hairdresser and then experiment with different products to see which works best for your particular hair type.

Try student classes at top salons. You can get excellent haircuts for a small fee. Call them for a schedule, and make sure it's clear what you're getting in advance.

Appreciate your own ethnic heritage and be creative with it. There are so many girls who want to change their natural hair type. But I say it's best to learn to love what you were born with. It's fine to experiment and try out new looks on your hair, but you don't want to get stuck having to constantly treat it (perming, relaxing, straightening, etc.), especially since that can be very damaging. It's cool to be creative sometimes, to transform your appearance with a new hairstyle, but I think it's more important to like what you have naturally.

Rip out pictures from magazines of cuts and styles you like and bring them to the salon.

Don't perm your young hair, especially if it is colored. If you want a curlier look than is natural, try a wig, or do something with curlers instead.

Coloring Tips

Don't only use one shampoo and/or conditioner all the time – your hair gets used to them and they become ineffective. Alternate different products that work for you.

Don't do home hair color – especially permanent color. Consult a hair color expert and decide with them.

Don't use Sun-In or alcohol in the sun as they dry out your hair. Use lemon juice mixed with water for subtle lightening, or chamomile tea.

Don't swim bare-headed in chlorinated water if you've had your hair colored, as it destroys the hair and the color. Wear a swim cap (I know they're ugly, but . . .).

Don't henna. It leaves a build-up that is difficult to remove if other color work is desired.

Cut first, before coloring, if you're going for a radical change.

See a color specialist if you've ruined your color at home. Don't try to fix it yourself.

DIFFERENT LOOKS ON SOME OF THE GIRLS, CLOCKWISE FROM TOP: KIRSTEN DUNST, IZMIRA
TAWFEEK, TING LUO, LeANN RIMES, AND SHARON ANYIMI.

She likes to say that at 18 months old she could sing better than she could talk. When she was five, she entered a talent show and won with her version of "Getting to Know You." "By the time I was six," says LeAnn Rimes, "my parents knew that I was really different." She was a two-week champion on *Star Search* at eight years old, and when she was 11 she cut her first record, *All That*, on an independent label.

By the time LeAnn was 13 – which was only a year ago – she recorded a song called "Blue," which was originally written for the late Patsy Cline (Cline died before she could record it). At first, LeAnn's father didn't want her to sing "Blue." He felt the lyrics were too mature, that a girl who had (and has) never gone on a date with a boy shouldn't be singing about lust with longing. But LeAnn, who is determined in the most straightforward, no-nonsense way, basically nagged him until he caved in.

When "Blue" was first played on the radio, country music stations were flooded with so many calls that they spun it once every couple of hours. It eventually reached the top 10 on the country music charts; her

CB

record, also called *Blue*, went to #1 on the country music charts and #3 on *Billboard*'s pop charts. She's spent the last several months on the road, and will spend much of this year touring, too.

LeAnn is the first to admit that country music is not exactly considered the hippest thing around – especially among people her age. (But she also admits that she really wouldn't know, as she has no friends her own age – she's home-tutored, and everyone she hangs around with works for her.) So she shops at Wet Seal and tries to cultivate a look that isn't stereotypically country. "I think the country-singer image started changing a couple of years ago," she says. "It was usually boots and jeans, and some artists, like Terry Clark, are dressing in country apparel still. But I think the music started to get more contemporary, and some of the pop people started coming over and listening to country music. And I think that the clothing has kind of changed, because a lot of the younger kids are getting into country, so you see the artists are dressing in the new hip stuff. I know for me, I love all the new 60s stuff that's coming out – some of

LeAnn

BY DANIEL PEEBLES

the pants that are not real bell bottom-y, but kind of flared."

In the liner notes to her CD, LeAnn thanks her grandparents, godparents, parents, agents, managers, songwriters, producers, bookers, backup musicians, God, and her makeup artists for "making me look good." "Sometimes makeup is a pain," she says, "because I usually have to touch it up two or three times a day. I've usually got a show that night, and maybe a couple of interviews. So I kind of get tired of it." She wears foundation, mascara, eyeliner, eye shadow, blush, and lipstick basically all the time.

LeAnn's been making up her face for shows since she was eight, and her mom taught her how to apply foundation and other basic stuff. "She would always use her hand to put base on, because it would blend real well, and that's what I've always done, use my hand instead of a sponge," says LeAnn. "And then, as I got into the business, I started working with makeup artists a lot, so that has helped me."

The two most important tricks she says she learned: "I never line my top lid with eyeliner. Never. I've got real small eyes, and that closes them off if I line the top of it. So I always line under the bottom. And you know when you put your lipstick on? Put your finger in your mouth, purse your lips, and then pull it

out, because that gets the lipstick off the inside of your mouth." For the most part, LeAnn favors natural tones, "like earth tones, kind of the brownish-looking stuff," she says. "I really don't like a lot of color in my makeup."

Her image may not be hipsterish, but she's got a look that works for her. On her CD cover, LeAnn's in a very demure, ladylike red dress, and while it's hardly cutting edge, she looks comfortable. But when she's photographed in stuff like a black-and-white striped scoop-neck and red vinyl vest (as she was for one magazine) with her carefully applied makeup; layered, fringy hair; and pearly pink manicure, she just doesn't look like a teenager. "I take that as a compliment," she says. "I do, because I do think I look a little bit older. And I'm very happy with the way I look. I love the clothes, and I think my makeup, my hair, everything – I think it's all fine." She pauses. "I guess all of us want to look older. Everybody tells me when I get to be 20, I'm going to want to be 14. But I don't think that's true." ❂

BELOW, LEFT TO RIGHT: AT AGE SEVEN; WITH PATSY MONTANA AT AGE EIGHT; AT HOME AT AGE FOUR; WITH SOME FANS IN HOUSTON IN 1996.

WHEN I FELT THE MOST BEAUTIFUL: AT THE CMA [COUNTRY MUSIC AWARDS].

I wash my hair: Daily with Hair Menders Moisturizing Shampoo followed by Redken Final Phase Conditioner.

MY DEEP, DARK BEAUTY SECRET: JUST BEING NATURAL – BEING ME!

My favorite homemade beauty concoction: Toothpaste on a pimple!

MY BIGGEST AS-YET-UNANSWERED BEAUTY QUESTION: HOW CAN I KEEP LOOKING GREAT AT 50!

Clockwise from top left: In Central Park, by CB, 1996; by Daniel Peebles; by CB, 1996.

WHO HAS TAUGHT ME ABOUT BEAUTY: MY MOM.

BEAUTY PRODUCT I'D LOVE TO FORGET: MUD MASKS AS THEY DRY MY FACE OUT!

I CAN'T LIVE WITHOUT MY: AVEDA LIQUID FOUNDATION.

Things I inherited I wish I hadn't/Things I inherited and love: I wish I didn't have dry skin. I love my eyelashes.

Marinelly Andrade has spent

the better part of her 18 years trying to fit in, trying not to be the nerd she says she was in sixth grade, or the Spanish girl trying to fit in at an all-white school, or the Spanish girl who was often accused of trying to actually be white. And though she doesn't care what people think anymore – she's usually dressed the way she is today, in jeans and a T-shirt, her straight black hair a thin sheath framing her makeup-free face – she believes that the way she looks *does* matter. "As sad as it is," she says, "I think that the way you look and the way you identify yourself is important to a lot of different people."

Up until she was seven, Marinelly lived in the Bronx with her parents and her two sisters. Her parents were very strict; her dad used to sit her down and debate issues with her, teach her how to pronounce multisyllabic words, help her think through tough math problems. When Marinelly was 11, her parents moved the family to Howard Beach, Queens. "That was pretty difficult at first," she says, "because it was mostly a white neighborhood. My mother is Puerto Rican and my father was Dominican, and when I moved to Howard Beach I had a really strong Spanish accent. A lot of the kids would laugh at that. For the first time in my life I got called 'spic.'" So she did everything she could possi-

bly think of to blend in. "It was horrible," she says now, shaking her head from side to side. "I would dress similar to everybody else. I would use certain terms that they would use, that I had never in my life heard – but just to fit in, I would use them. And that was really horrible, because I knew it wasn't me, and I thought, What am I trying to do here?"

She was only in Howard Beach for a year when her father passed away. The family picked up and moved to Jamaica, another neighborhood in Queens. "I totally transformed again!" she says with a laugh. "And that was the total opposite of Howard Beach – a lot of black and Indian people live there. And, I mean, a lot of people thought I *was* white, and I'm like, 'No way!' It's like, if they thought I *was* white, that presented a problem, but when they found

Marinelly Andrade

Activist
18 years old
Born and lives in New York, U.S.A.

Opposite: Collage by Marinelly, featuring a self-portrait, 1996.

out I wasn't, it was like, 'Oh, it's okay,' you know?" And Marinelly – who had won a two-week scholarship to study at Adelphi University when she was in the sixth grade – began to have serious trouble at school. "It got harder after my dad passed away," she says, "because from there I didn't have that strong role model, that backbone, that support. That's when I started, you know, flunking math, because I didn't have that spark. And there was a whole junior high issue where you're changing classes and, you know, everybody already had their group of friends. I had no friends. I had no one to talk to."

In her second year of junior high, Marinelly met her first boyfriend; she was 13, he was 17, and, needless to say, her mother did not approve of who she was see-

ing or the changes she was going through. "I wasn't allowed to wear makeup," she says conspiratorially, "so I used to sneak it on, like, right before school, and take it off right after school, before I got home. If you see a picture of me when I was 12 and then you see a picture of me when I was 13, you'd think, Oh my God, what happened? I totally changed during that year. When I was 13, that's when I wore eyeliner, I wore mascara, I wore lipstick, I did my nails. I did my nails like three times a day. I had the hair spray; I used to do all these weird, freaky styles on my hair. Forget it. My style was totally important to me back then because of the people around me. Their perception of me was so important to me that I would just do anything, you know, to fit in. That was the whole issue for me." She

WHEN I FELT THE LEAST BEAUTIFUL: WHEN MY HEART GOT BROKEN BY A PREVIOUS LOVER.

My deep, dark beauty secret: Love yourself for who you are and you'll be beautiful!!

BEAUTY TO ME IS...

MY FAMILY.

AND HOW WE STAYED TOGETHER EVEN A
DAY

A FRIENDSHIP THAT

7 YEAR

u color it
purple
blue
green
yellow
orange
red
GAY PRIDE...
PRID

MY NIECE...

FOR A PET!...

women

MY BODY ART...

HAVING MY OWN FAMILY
IN THE FUTURE!

POetry...

AGE EIGHT

looks down at the floor. "It's so funny when I look back," she says. "I don't even paint my nails anymore."

Around the same time, Marinelly decided to quit school. "To this day I regret it. But again, I was having a lot of problems at home, and I didn't fit in in high school. I already came out, and . . . I probably only had two friends in high school. I really thought that I did not fit in there," she says firmly. "I found myself cutting school just to go to the park, or just to stay home and just to spend time with myself. I couldn't deal with it. It was just really horrible; it was a horrible experience." Her mom was about to have an aneurysm at this point. "Oh, forget it," says Marinelly. "She was very surprised because I was her little, like, angel daughter, you know? She wasn't too pleased." But Marinelly promised to get her GED, and her mom relented. "She felt, you know, 'If this is what you're going to do, fine; if you regret it later, you'll know why.'"

Marinelly says she didn't go through a particularly traumatic experience or have any kind of epiphany about her sexuality, but for a month, she says, she felt "really confused." She hooked herself up with a couple of organizations for gay and lesbian youth that she found through local hot-lines. "Once I started meeting other gay people," she says, "I was just like, 'Oh, forget it, this is me!'" She got active in outreach programs and began interning at the Gay Men's Health Crisis.

After coming out to her family and friends, Marinelly says she began paying even more attention to her looks than she had before. "My biggest change period was when I turned 16," she says. "I think the first part of it was my clothing. I used to wear tight pants all the time, or really, really baggy pants, and just carry that

I FREAK OUT IF I LEAVE HOME WITHOUT MY: TOOTHBRUSH AND
TOOTHPASTE; VANILLA-FLAVORED LIP BALM.

WHEN I FELT THE MOST BEAUTIFUL: WHEN I SPOKE IN FRONT OF
HUNDREDS OF PEOPLE AT THE GAY & LESBIAN RALLY.

CB

OPPOSITE PAGE AND THIS PAGE, LOWER TOP ROW, LEFT TO RIGHT: AGE 10; AGE 15; WITH
HER FATHER AT SIX MONTHS; AGE 17. BOTTOM ROW, LEFT TO RIGHT: AGE 14; MARINELLY
(CENTER) WITH HER SISTERS ANANERY AND JEANNIE; AGE ONE.

look. Then it changed to bell-bottoms and T-shirts, you know?" And Marinelly chopped all her hair off. "That was wonderful," she says. "Just a relief. Because I had never been given authorization to cut my hair. I carried that, the short-hair look, for a year. I colored it purple, and that was fun. And last summer I got my nose pierced, and then my belly, and then my eyebrow. I got my first tattoo when I was 16 – it kind of looks like a sun."

Today Marinelly volunteers for the National Abortion Rights Action League and for the Third Wave Fund, a grantmaking organization for women ages 15 – 30; and helps produce a cable-access show targeted to gay and lesbian kids. But she also thinks she wants to be a doctor, and now holds down a job in a doctor's office, which she loves. "He's a gastroenterologist – it took me a month to learn how to say that!" she laughs. "But it's funny, because this is my struggle: I'm expected to wear nice suits and shoes, and take off all body piercings, you know? And it's like, 'Oh my God, this is so uncomfortable,' but it's something I have to do in order to earn money. So before I leave work, if I'm going to head downtown later, I bring some clothes with me and I change completely into, like, my jeans, my T-shirt, and I put back my earrings. It's weird – I'm going through that stage right now where I want to present myself as an adult but I want to have fun at the same time. And they're both colliding right now."

Marinelly also says that she's never been more comfortable with herself since she quit trying so hard to fit in. "I'm happy with who I am," she says. "I don't think that I'd be as confident as I am now if I didn't feel like I was beautiful. And I don't

CB

think beauty is so much about looks. It's just the way you carry yourself. And I'm happy with the way I carry myself." She still lives in Queens with her mom, and says they're superclose – although her mom still has problems with Marinelly's sexuality. "She doesn't want to acknowledge it," she says. "She knows, but she just doesn't care. That's the way she wants to

deal with it for now. But I'll accept that till she's ready to talk to me about it or whatever." She thinks for a moment. "I may change, you know," she says. "Maybe in a couple of years I'll feel the need to have no more body piercings, no more tattoos. I haven't gotten any more tattoos because I haven't found something that really means something. Like the one on my back, it's a Celtic design that symbolizes peace, and when you look at it, it's like a triangle, but it's like a little maze. And I figure that's what my life is. You have difficult times and you have times that are easy, but you just go do the things you have to do. It's a maze." 🌑

How long it takes me to get ready for school: The way I look every day is equal to the way I feel. So I usually dress to what I'm feeling. It takes me about 30 minutes to get dressed. I don't wear makeup except for lipstick occasionally.

AGE TWO

THE BEST BEAUTY TRICKS I'VE LEARNED: FORGET ABOUT MAKEUP. STICK WITH LIP BALM AND FACE LOTION AND LOVE YOURSELF. REMEMBER BEAUTY IS INTERNAL. BEAUTY IS JUDGED BY YOUR HEART!

THINGS I INHERITED AND LOVE: MY HEIGHT, 5'8", AND MY STRAIGHT BROWN HAIR.

Who has taught me about beauty: I've always defined beauty as something internal. My definition is someone who is at peace with themselves, happy, and open-minded. I learned all this by myself but my friend and sisters helped influence this attitude. Also that beauty is being able to speak your mind and express yourself.

MARTINA

Martina Hingis
Tennis Player
16 years old
Born in Czechoslovakia
Lives in Switzerland

I'VE BEEN SITTING IN THE LOBBY of the UN Plaza Hotel in midtown Manhattan for a half hour, waiting for Martina Hingis to show up. I'm growing a little restless. I know that she has a flight to catch in little over an hour, and if she doesn't show up soon I'm going to miss my only chance to meet her in person. Then, out of the corner of my eye, I notice a flurry of activity at the hotel's entrance. Martina has arrived. I stand up and wave, and she dashes over to me, full of apologies. She's sorry she's late, she explains, but she was having her pictures done for this book. Plus she just finished competing in an exhausting tournament yesterday (she lost, she says with a smile) and has to catch a flight ✈ to Australia, where she will compete in yet another tournament. She asks if I mind if we squeeze in our talk now, and I tell her it's fine, of course. She plops in an overstuffed chair and takes a deep breath, then laughs.

This is Martina's life, and she finds it kind of amusing. I'm impressed at how cheerful and eager she is to talk, especially since she played yesterday's match in a fair amount of pain. "I had cramps and I couldn't really move – I couldn't run on the court," she tells me. "It was really pretty funny. You know, I had the chance to beat Steffi [Graf], and I knew, yeah, I can't really move anymore, so it wasn't very easy to play. But she wasn't very healthy either – she had a knee and a back injury. But, I mean, she's a little bit older and more experienced, so she just handled it better."

At 16, Martina is ranked 4th in the world among female tennis players. (She's also the youngest player in history to win a junior Grand Slam title.) Her mother, who herself was a professional tennis player in her native Czechoslovakia, named her daughter after Martina Navratilova, and, when her daughter was two, fashioned a makeshift tennis racket out of pieces of her toddler's crib. "My mom played until she got pregnant with me," says Martina. "She was 23 years old, and she stopped playing tennis herself. So then she started to play with me." Martina was, she says, two years old when she had her first lesson. When she was eight, she and her mother moved to ※ Switzerland; even though Martina spoke neither German nor English, she picked up both languages quickly. And though she spent most of her time on the court, she got near-perfect grades.

"I wasn't really, really talented," Martina continues. "I think it's just hard work. Maybe it became a talent, but I don't think it's only talent or whatever. It's just hard work; practicing every day, or doing something every day for tennis. The other kids, they were on the street and they would have fun there, and I was always on the court. And I was happy with that."

That is where Martina seems most at home. In the cab on the way to the hotel, I had been reading about Martina's defeat in her match the day before, but all the papers had to say was that it was a minor setback and pretty much irrelevant considering her prodigious ability. Even Steffi Graf had said that Martina was "definitely the player to watch." And a sports editor I know had been telling me that Martina was a double threat not just because of her amazing ability, but because there aren't enough young, attractive female athletes to focus on. I ask her how she feels about this. "Well," she begins, "I like when people talk about me like that. It's nice to hear, you know, you have a nice game

and a nice smile on the court." But in the next breath she tells me that she thinks there's a huge difference between the way male and female athletes are covered by the press. "Men are always easier – everyone looks to you, like, 'Yeah, you're a big hero,' or something," Martina says. "And females, they just have to be feminine on the court and just – like, the crowd laughs if someone like McEnroe throws his racket over the fence or something, but a female, you always have to be very quiet." She laughs. Martina's got no problem expressing her emotions on the court.

She also tells me that she puts a lot of thought into what she wears when she competes; she compares the court to ♟ theater. "You're in front of a big crowd, and people are watching you, so, I mean, my mom always wanted to have me in a nice skirt." So Martina, who says she's into fashion "a lot," gets a bunch of new outfits for every season (in tennis, there are three). She likes to wear a lot of color (she tells me not many tennis players wear

BY ALESE AND MORTON PECHTER

all white anymore), and wants to look as elegant as she can while pummeling an opponent. And when she's not on the court she wears basic stuff, like jeans, during the day, but loves to get dressed up at night. "I like a lot of black things," she says, "because I just think the color is elegant and it's always nice. And things that fit on

BY ALESE AND MORTON PECHTER

your body," she continues. "I like Moschino. I saw a very nice dress from Chloe, from the collection of Lagerfeld – it was very, like, tight, but you could use it for a ball or something. It's very simple. The simplest things are sometimes the nicest."

Traveling as much as she does, Martina has picked up what she thinks are basic differences in the way Americans and Europeans dress. "The Americans, they like to be casual, like sloppy sometimes," she says without a trace of disparagement. (Martina herself is wearing a pair of faded blue jeans and a nondescript blue sweatshirt.) "I think in Europe the level is higher, like in the cities. More elegant. The people there wear nice dresses. But, you know, it depends on the person, I think. You have both sides in America and in Europe."

Martina also tells me that she loves makeup almost as much as she loves fashion, but that she can't wear it on the court – and she plays, she guesses, about

350 days out of the year. She doesn't have a lot of time to fuss over her hair either, so she just recently lopped it all off. "It was a big change, you know – there was nothing there anymore!" she exclaims. "But it's easier this way, I don't have to deal with it anymore." As for makeup, "I like it if someone else does it instead of doing it myself," she says. "I'm 16, and I don't really know how to do it. I just like a very natural look, maybe some eyeliner." Like most of the girls I talked to for this book, Martina's favorite feature is her eyes. "You know, my mother has very blue eyes, and when I was little I had a lot more blue in my eyes," she says. "Now it's like a mixture between green and blue and gray, so it's like . . ." She laughs. "But I think the eyes have a lot of power – there comes a lot of energy out of the eyes."

If and when she stops playing tennis, Martina says she wants to model. "But I have a chance to do it with my tennis, too," she says. "My mom always told me to look good on the court, expressing yourself, showing your emotions. I mean, I just throw my racket away sometimes if I'm angry with myself, or just talk to myself, 'Hey, concentrate!'" Martina thinks that not hiding how she's feeling at a particular moment is part of the reason people connect with her. "I think other girls could be like that, too," she says. "Like, Steffi is a very nice person, but she just doesn't show anything on the court. And Gabriela Sabatini – she is a great, great athlete, and one who has a great personality." Martina gets distracted; she looks like she's just remembered something. Glancing at her watch, she apologizes to me again, saying she's got to go or she'll miss her flight. She picks up her bags and her racket. "I mean, my mom always told me to show my emotions on the court," she concludes. "To show how you are." And she's out the door.

AGE TWO

AGE NINE

AGE SEVEN

Monica

R&B Singer

16 years old

Born and lives in Georgia, U.S.A.

MONICA ARNOLD IS 16 years old. ♪ She's been singing, she likes to say, since before she knew how to talk. When she was nine, her aunt Laura entered her in a church-sponsored pageant in Atlanta. She remembers wearing a red velvet dress, she remembers singing "The Greatest Love of All," and remembers being crowned. ♛

Now she goes only by her first name. She says that she likes to keep Monica, the Person, and Monica, the Entertainer, "combined as one." She explains it this way: "They can be two different people almost. So I try to keep Monica in check – the person, not the entertainer. I'm not saying I've got, like, these split personalities going on, but when I'm in public I've got to act one way, and when I'm at home I've got to act another way. I want to be me all of the time."

At the age of 11, as she was making her way through the local talent-show circuit – singing "The Greatest Love of All" every time – a man named Kevin Wales approached her. He thought Monica should meet Dallas Austin, a writer and producer who had worked with Madonna and Boyz II Men. So she sang for Dallas. "I think if I had known who he was and the different things he had done and produced, I would have been a little nervous," she says now. "So it worked out for the better, because it gave me the chance to show my full abilities."

Dallas wrote a song for Monica called "Don't Take It Personal," which turned out to be a huge hit – it eventually went to number one on the R&B charts, and MTV ran the video into the ground. She was 14 then, and this was how she described the song at the time: "It has kind of a deep message that lets guys know it's not all about them, that sometimes girls need time for themselves. Although I don't date yet, I know I wouldn't want a man up under me 24-7. I might love him, but these are the 90s, and I also have to have a life of my own. Hey, when I need my space he's gonna have to respect that – or he's got to step."

Monica's parents got divorced when she was five. She lives in Atlanta with her mom – who works for Delta Airlines, and her stepfather – who's a Methodist preacher. She has two younger brothers. Monica says she grew to love Dallas as a father, and now actually calls him Daddy. She says that her whole family is okay with that, except her birth father. "He probably is not comfortable with the situation," Monica admits. "But he has to look at the circumstances, and he can only accept it. I have been raised by two people other than himself, so he can't really dispute the issue."

In her freshman year of high school, Monica decided she should leave and get a tutor so she could go out on the road, opening for TLC and co-headlining with the group Immature. It was her first tour, but she says she wasn't nervous at all, that she's always been very comfortable on-stage. Her adrenaline surges and at times she feels like she's not even in her own body. But she does get worn down – she has asthma, and it's gotten progressively worse, sometimes requiring special medical attention. "That's been difficult," she says. She has to watch her diet, and when the weather changes, she has to be extra careful.

"I try to encourage everyone, especially teenagers, to address their medical problems instead of ignoring them," she says. "I give motivational talks to teens in high schools, churches, and for a variety of other organizations. I stress that what I do is not all glamorous, but a lot of hard work too, and that it's very important that I stay healthy, because if I'm sick, either I can't perform my best, which I really don't like, or I can't perform at all. I tell people to get regular check-ups, then follow-ups as needed. I've had various types of

sickness in my family, and you'll be surprised how important it is to catch problems early. It is often the difference between life and death."

When Monica feels stressed or pressured, she likes to go to L.A. "I go see Dallas and my friends," she says. "You know, he just bought me a ⊛ Benz for my 16th birthday, and my car keeps me happy when it comes to drama. I will get in my car, and just ride and just think. The pager is probably going off, the cellular phone is definitely ringing, and I just ignore them all." And, of course, she shops. She's into Naughty by Nature gear, Tommy Hilfiger, and Nike, but "when it's time to step out," she says, "we want to step all the way out. I love gowns – I love Versace, Dolce & Gabbana, Prada, and DKNY things. And I love heels. I've always been able to walk in them, and I've always loved to be dressed up." Yet Monica loathes makeup. "I hate the feeling," she groans. "My complexion, fortunately, even through puberty, has been clear, and I haven't had a problem

I WASH MY HAIR: EVERY THREE DAYS.

with my skin. To have to wear all that makeup to protect my skin from the stage lights and stuff bothers me. If you ever catch me just running around, you will never see me with any more than lipstick on – MAC 's Odyssey or Media."

This is not to say that she doesn't care about the way she looks. "I always felt," she says, "that if you're a female, you should comb your hair and just do certain things, you know? I know some women who are like, 'Oh, I don't feel like it,' who get out of bed and leave without combing their hair, not even putting on a hat with something to match it! But I've always been that way. That's just me – not just because of Monica the Entertainer." Looking your best at all times is important, Monica believes, because "it builds your self-esteem. Brand names don't matter – as long as you keep your clothes clean and neat, then you can take pride in yourself."

As Monica does. "I feel like [we] women should be respected, those of us who have done things for ourselves, who don't just sit there and take men's money, and all of the things that men rap about so often." When I ask her how she feels about women being treated like sex objects in so many videos, she says, "If you are the woman overexposing your body in

Who has taught me about beauty: Gwyniss.

I CAN'T LIVE WITHOUT MY: MAC LIPLINER.

BEAUTY PRODUCT I'D LOVE TO FORGET: MASCARA.

I FELT THE MOST BEAUTIFUL/LEAST BEAUTIFUL: NOW/AS A KID.

THE BEST BEAUTY TRICKS I'VE LEARNED: NOT TO USE MASCARA; AND ON THE LIPS,
USE LIPLINER AND FILL IN WITH YOUR LIPSTICK.

BY SAM JONES

AT THREE AND A HALF MONTHS

"Don't Take It Personal"
by Dallas Austin

It's just one of them days
When I wanna be your love
It's just one of them days
When I gotta be all alone
It's just one of them things
Don't take it personal

Just wanna be all alone
And think I treat you wrong

I wanna take some time out
To think things through
I know it always feels like
I'm doing you wrong
But it's all in love in you

So understand that I'm only in love
You're the only one I need
So have no thought
That I want to leave
And baby trust me please

Chorus
Just one of them days
That a girl goes through
When I'm angry inside
Don't wanna take it out on you
Just one of them things
Don't take it personal
Just wanna be all alone
And you think I think you wrong
Don't take it personal
Baby, baby, baby, baby
Don't take it personal

I sit and think about
Everything we do
As I find myself in misery
And that ain't cool

And now I really wanna be with you
The whole way through
'Cause the way you make me feel inside
Must be confused

As I swing back
It's not because of you
I never want you to be insecure

So won't you understand
That I'm only in love
You're the only one I need
I'll be there for you
When you need me boy
So baby don't you leave

Just one of them days
That a girl goes through
When I'm angry inside
Don't wanna take it out on you
Just one of them things
Don't take it personal
Just wanna be all alone
And you think I treat you wrong

MY DEEP, DARK BEAUTY SECRETS: DEEP CLEANSING, MOISTURIZING FAITHFULLY, DRINK PLENTY OF WATER, EAT HEALTHILY.

IF YOU GAVE ME $100 TO SPEND ON BEAUTY EXCITEMENT, I'D BUY: A DAY AT CARTER BARNES.

the video, then you put yourself in that predicament. Nobody made you do anything. And men have their own perceptions of women. I've seen some of the women that disrespect themselves, and some of the rappers that hang around me sit down and write about them. So I can't knock them about what they write, because the women put themselves in that position."

For the most part, Monica says she likes being famous. "When I'm recognized in different cities," she says, "I'm like, 'Okay, well, obviously I'm in rotation here' or 'People love me here.' I accept being a role model. When I read my fan mail, and I hear them talking about how they cut their hair when they saw my haircut or just . . . when I call the hospital, when I call a child who's been sick for weeks, and all of a sudden her days are brightened – I take that to heart."

Monica is not insecure, she says. Ever. "I try not to be insecure about *anything*," she says. "That word is not even in my vocabulary." She does have advice for all of us, however, on how not to be insecure or get jealous or worry over the way we look. "Always think of *self first*," she says firmly. "I know it sounds selfish, but when you do, you save yourself a lot of heartache. Deal with self. Think about self. If you're pleased with yourself, and you embed that in your brain, it's going to get to the point ☞ where no one can take that away from you – not a man, or a woman." That lesson, she says, came from her mother. "She is a solid teacher," says Monica proudly. "If I would have been crippled in a fire or a car accident, I still would have been able to deal with self. I was always taught to be pleased with self. And I always *was* pleased with self." ❂

Just one of them days
Just one of them days
That a girl goes through
When I'm angry inside
Don't wanna take it out on you

Just one of them things
Don't take it personal
I just wanna be all alone
When you think I treat you wrong
Don't take it personal
Baby, baby, baby, baby
Don't take it personal

Just one of them days
That a girl goes through
When I'm angry inside
Don't wanna take it out on you
Just one of them things
Don't take it personal
Just wanna be all alone
And you think I treat you wrong

Don't take it personal

BY QUINN HOOD

BY DARRELL P. LANE

ABOVE, TOP: MONICA WITH DALLAS AUSTIN. BOTTOM: WITH HER BROTHER MONTEZ.

BY MATTHEW JORDAN SMITH

WITH HER MOM ON HER FIRST BIRTHDAY

Natalie Portman

Actress
15 years old
Born in Israel
Lives in New York, U.S.A.

NATALIE PORTMAN ARRIVES at my apartment early Saturday morning, takes off her coat, and sinks into an armchair. In her long-sleeved white pullover, tailored navy trousers, chunky-heeled loafers, and what appears to be no makeup, Natalie looks her age – 15 – but seems older in a self-possessed way.

We start talking about what she feels is an in-between stage of her life. Like just about every teenager I've ever met, she dislikes the word "teen." "You go through these phases – one second you're a child, the next you're a woman. I'm still very kid-like. I like playing."

When I comment on the fact that she is not wearing any makeup, Natalie explains she actually is. "I usually wear cover-up and Chapstick – those are my basics."

The truth is, even though Natalie has always felt confident about her appearance, she doesn't place much importance on physical beauty, in herself or other people. "I think self-confidence is such a part of beauty," she says. "My whole family is beautiful because they're confident and intelligent. All of my really close friends are so beautiful," she continues. "Many of them are really, really beautiful externally and internally. It's not like one of my criteria, like I put out an ad – 'Pretty people please apply,'" she explains. "But everyone seems to think my friends are beautiful. When you look at them you can tell they're good people from the way they act and the way they feel about themselves and other people. If you don't think you're a beautiful person, then other people won't either."

But she has always had to deal with the attention her looks bring her. When she was nine, Natalie was hanging out in a pizza parlor in her Long Island neighborhood when a Revlon executive approached her and asked her if she would like to be a model. Natalie turned down that offer, but decided to pursue acting. When she was 11, she was cast in her first film – *The Professional*, in which she played a young girl who witnesses her family's murder. Last year she starred in designer Isaac Mizrahi's "Inside every woman there's a star" ad campaign

This page, top row, left to right: With her dad; with her dad in Israel; at age five; at age six; at age 10. Center of page, top: By Cliff Watts/Botaish Group; bottom: at age 13. Opposite page: By Eika Aoshima/Botaish Group.

for his ISAAC line (the photographs fueled constant comparisons with Audrey Hepburn). She then received widespread acclaim for her portrayal of "Marty" in the film *Beautiful Girls*.

Many girls would love to look like Natalie, so I ask her to let others know if there are appearance issues she deals with. She tells me her hair has caused problems ever since she was seven and got a haircut and wound up with these "big banana curls." For photos, Natalie's hair is usually straightened using a blow-dryer. "It takes me hours to blow-dry my hair," she says. "My hair's not just curly – it's crazy curly. It's as if it hasn't decided what to do. It's a mess. For school, I just pull it back into a ponytail.

"People always tell me I'm cute," Natalie continues. "When a guy tells me I'm cute, it's not something desirable. Cute is more like what you want your pet to be."

Also, certain aspects of being in "the business," as Natalie refers to her movie career, can't help but make her slightly self-conscious of her looks. "When I went to see *Mars Attacks*, my face became 10 feet tall and a pimple that was so small seemed huge, like a mosaic," she says. "Or, if I'm having a bad hair day, it's not something personal. It's something that's going to be in a magazine."

Since Natalie was 11, she's worked with hair and makeup artists. "Probably the best beauty tip I ever learned was to put Vaseline on my eyelashes. It makes them darker. And at the movies, if you don't know if it's going to be sad, it's great if you don't want mascara running down your face." When she goes out, Natalie generally just wears lip gloss and blush. If she goes to a premiere for a film she is in, she goes to a makeup artist, because of all the paparazzi photos.

Natalie has been styled in vastly different ways from film to film. "I think the way a character looks is so important for a film, because it really tells you so much about who the character is. In *The Professional*, I had a very sleek, French haircut, which was appropriate for the mood of the film. Then, in *Beautiful Girls*, I was dressed like a normal kid, an average suburban girl."

In her own suburban girl life, Natalie's style is simple. "At school I'm really a comfortable dresser," she says. "I just need to be in clothes I can get through class in." So it's a lot of jeans, cords, sweaters, and tees. However, she does have a couple of little fashion quirks. After wrapping up *The Professional*, Natalie could be seen around her hometown wearing the same heavy brown boots she'd worn for the character of Mathilda in the

mother's really, really beautiful. She's a really strong woman, she's been through a lot, and she's maintained a real great spirit with her. I love looking at pictures of her when she first came to Israel in the 1930s and the 40s. She was so glamorous, with her hair and her suits."

Another figure Natalie admires is Anne Frank – when she was 13, she decided she was going to play her, and started looking for potential projects. This fall, Natalie is portraying Anne in a Broadway play. "I think because Anne didn't realize anyone was going to read her diary, it's the most honest thing," Natalie says. "Her story represents many things wrong about the world and her life represents everything that's right about life."

film. "I often wear my shoes from the movies, because they are the only things that don't get recognized."

Natalie also loves to carry around all these quirky little bags. "I think purses are so grown-up, adult, so I have five or six little bags," she explains. "I have my Sea World bag I used at camp, my Sesame Street backpack for dance, and my penguin bag someone brought me from Japan. It's a funny way to show your personality without being uncomfortable," she adds. "I tend to go for plain clothes and little, crazy bags."

While her beauty routine and clothing style may both be fairly simple, Natalie knows her looks are somewhat exotic. That's because of her background. Part of her extended family is from Israel, where Natalie lived until the age of three. "I look a lot like my family and I have Mediterranean features," she says. "Right now I'm tan, so I feel so Israeli. I like having something special about me. I'm not that average blond-haired, blue-eyed American girl." She continues, "My grand-

AT AGE FOUR

Like the Franks, many of Natalie's family members did not survive the Holocaust. Natalie turns gravely serious when she talks about this aspect of her heritage. "There is a spirit that Israelis have," Natalie explains. "We've been through so much – not me personally – but there are people who have sacrificed so much so I can be alive today. The spirit that goes along with being Israeli is kind of a weight placed on you that you must enjoy, and you appreciate life because of it. My people in general, have fought so hard that it gives me a sense of responsibility," Natalie continues. "Jews have learned to excel despite hardship. We have learned that life should not be wasted, and the importance of education."

Which is what Natalie plans to keep doing through her acting. "My family's really pleased," she says. "But I think they're still working on making me a doctor." ⚽

Oksana Baiul was three and a half years old

the first time her looks were slagged. "I was pleasantly plump," she recalls, grimacing a little. "I don't want to say about myself I was fat, but I was a big girl, you know? And my mom had dreams – she wanted me to be a ballet dancer. But my grandfather said, 'She's too fat to be a ballet dancer.'" So Oksana's mother took her down to a skating rink. "I lost my weight," says Oksana, matter-of-factly. "Then when I was seven, my mother asked me, 'Do you want to go to ballet school?' And then I said, 'No. I love figure skating.'"

Oksana grew up in Dnepropetrovsk, a small town in the Ukraine. An only child, her parents divorced when she was two, and she never saw her father again. Her grandparents died when she was just 10; then, when she was 14, her mother died of cancer. Finally, her coach took off for Canada, promising he'd return. He didn't. "It was a very hard situation," she says quietly. "I didn't have anybody. Anybody. Nobody cared about me. I was by myself, and I didn't know what to do. So then I say, 'Okay, I have to go somewhere and do something with myself.' Because I was freaked."

Her friend Viktor Petrenko ("He is very big – he won the Olympic Games in 1992," she says) convinced his coach, a woman named Galina, to train Oksana. "I find Galina," says Oksana, "and then I feel I found a second family for me really." Galina quickly threw her into an exhausting, five-hour-a-day training schedule. "I see the results in one year," says Oksana, eyebrows raised, head bobbing slowly.

By the time she was 16, she was ready to compete in the 1994 Winter Olympics, but she was too poor to afford the kind of costume she coveted. So her coach's mother hand-stitched one to her specifications: a shiny, bubble gum–pink confection with fuzzy white epaulets. It was a little over-the-top – not to mention her Technicolor makeup, which Oksana applied with quite a heavy hand – but in a way, it was totally perfect, because it was a 16-year-old Ukrainian girl's idea of what constituted glamour.

"Now I have special people who work with me on the costumes," says Oksana, who claims that her taste has matured a bit since then. She

Oksana Baiul
Olympic Gold Medalist Figure Skater
18 years old
Born in Dnepropetrovsk, Ukraine
Lives in Connecticut, U.S.A.

BY DAVE BLACK

still sketches rough designs and hands them over to seamstresses, along with specific instructions. "If I go into a store and buy a costume, it's just a suit for me. Okay? I didn't put anything into that costume. What I do, making my costumes – I want to put a little bit of my heart into it, so I don't feel like it's not my idea."

As you all know, Oksana floored the judges at the 1994 Winter Olympics with her technical proficiency and won the gold medal, beating out America's sweetheart, Nancy Kerrigan. Though Kerrigan had been knee-bashed only weeks before, Oksana skated with her own slightly less press-worthy injury: the day before the Olympics, during rehearsal, Oksana slammed into a fellow skater and slashed her right leg open. The doctors stitched her up, then shot up her leg with a painkiller. "I swear to God, it was so bad," she admits now. "I went the next day to practice and then I was freaked because I couldn't do anything. I had the worst practice in my whole entire life, and I would start crying and my coach was like, 'Well, Oksana, you have to make decisions right now.'" Actually, her coach really wanted her to sit out the games, but Oksana wouldn't listen. "I was working so hard for that time, and I just thought, I have to skate, and I don't care if I will win. And my coach, she's like, 'What about if your pain starts getting worse and worse?' and I say, 'Well, I don't

know.'" She pauses. "Then she said, 'Okay. I guess your mom, she's going to help you.' Those are the only words I do remember. And I go out there and I started doing my program and everything goes right and right and right, and when I was done my coach was like, 'Oksana, don't cry, don't cry, please. Just sit here and keep smiling. Please try to do that.'" She smiles broadly. "And then it came, you know, the marks, and then I start crying because I can't believe, you know . . . that I did it."

Suddenly, she was a celebrity. President Clinton invited her to the White House; Barbara Walters interviewed her on one of those annual 10 Most Fascinating People specials; there was even the biographical TV movie with the cloying title *A Promise Kept: The Oksana Baiul Story*. "It was a huge deal," she says of her win. "I was the first girl to win Olympic gold for Ukraine." Still, in 1994, Oksana decided to move to Connecticut. "Ukraine was such a nightmare because we don't have ice machines, we don't have Zambonis, we don't have room for skating – we don't have normal conditions, you know? So Galina has a very, very

BY DAVE BLACK

Something I inherited and love: I inherited my father's character, his spirit.

BY DANIELA FEDERICI

What's in my medicine cabinet: Moisturizer and toner for my face, plus several different types of sports creams for sore muscles.

close friend named Bob, and he called her and said, 'Listen, Galina, I find a guy, he's very wealthy and he just wants to build the ice rink for Oksana and Viktor so that she can move here and practice in here.' So that's why we move here." (At the time, she spoke almost no English; she picked up most of it by watching *Melrose Place* and *Beverly Hills, 90210*.) ♣

Oksana lives alone in a swanky Connecticut condo ("But I do always have somebody with me, because sometimes I'm scared to be by myself"). She still practices every day, and goes out on tour regularly with other skaters. In her free time she likes going into New York City – at least once every couple of weeks – where she gorges herself on Russian food ("I'm eating everything – Oksana likes chocolate too much to diet"), and heads down to her favorite makeup shop. "I am sick about makeup," she says, rolling her eyes. "I have every single color, because every day I put my makeup on differently. All the time when I'm going to the MAC store I'm like, 'I want that and that and that.' And sometimes, I come home and I open up all the boxes and I'm like, 'Oh, okay, I do have that color.'" Some days Oksana makes her eyes all smoky and dramatic. Others, she opts for no color except for bold lipstick, like Russian Red. She says she's seri-

My deep, dark beauty secret: It's actually an old Russian beauty secret. You take some eucalyptus and heat it up in a pot of water. After it cools, you pour the water into ice cube trays. Once the water freezes, you can use the ice cubes for your skin. I like to make a batch of these ice cubes and rub one on my face each morning to freshen my skin.

I FREAK OUT IF I LEAVE HOME WITHOUT MY: PRESSED POWDER.

BY DANIELA FEDERICI

If you gave me $100 to spend on beauty excitement, I'd buy: A facial or a massage.

Something I inherited I wish I hadn't: Nothing. I am really happy about all my features.

ously considering a later career as a makeup artist. "I can sit a person down in front of me and I think, That color will look good on her," she says proudly. "I don't use tricks – I just put on what I feel is right."

And though she's picked up tips from makeup artists (stuff like how to groom her eyebrows and conceal under-eye circles), she slacks off a lot of the time. For one thing, she wears makeup every day – foundation and powder are mainstays – but doesn't always wash her face at night. "That's why my skin is so bad," she remarks bashfully. (It's not really, a zit or two is all I can see.) And she has forever renounced the at-home, DIY dye job. "I went into some CVS store with Eddie, my friend – it was midnight – and said, 'I want to dye my hair,' and Eddie said, 'Oksana, it's not a good idea.

Don't do it.'" At the time, she was a strawberry blond, which was not her natural shade either. But she had never heard the rule about not dumping one color on top of another, or, if she had, she didn't care. Her hair turned green overnight. "It was so bad I was crying. My friend Jodie came over and started laughing so hard she was crying. She says, 'You look like some punk.' So I went to some hairdresser to have it fixed, and he was laughing. He was like, 'I can picture you on the ice with this green color and white dress. It would look so good.'" Even Oksana is laughing now. ⚘

These days she's working on a more sophisticated look. "I remember my thinking when I was 15 years old – right now, I will be 19, and it's such a huge difference. I'm sorry, but I will not look 16 forever."

Today she's wearing a tailored, career-woman beige suit by Jil Stuart; she usually goes for funkier stuff by Prada and Cynthia Rowley. "I have three closets in my house and they're all filled with clothes," says Oksana, clearly not pleased with herself. (She remembers her mother stitching almost all their clothing by hand because they were so poor.) "I don't need a lot like I do have right now. It's stupid to have so much clothes like I do. So I send a lot of stuff to my friends back in Ukraine. They were calling me and saying, 'Oh my God, we've never seen such beautiful dresses!' and they were saying ten thousand times thank you." While she's been loud and animated throughout our conversation, now she sounds almost as if she's talking to herself. She stares at the floor. "And I'm

MY BIGGEST AS-YET-UNANSWERED BEAUTY QUESTION: I WISH SOMEONE
WOULD TELL ME HOW TO GET RID OF SKIN BREAKOUTS RIGHT AWAY. THEY
ALWAYS HAPPEN AT THE WORST TIMES.

BEAUTY PRODUCT I'D LOVE TO FORGET: ONCE I BOUGHT A HAIR
PRODUCT THAT TURNED MY HAIR GREEN. IT WAS TERRIBLE.

saying, 'You don't have to say thank you. You don't have to say that because I've been in the same situation as you are right now and I know how painful it is when you want something and you can't buy it." She pauses. "You know, right now I'm changing — my hair, my makeup, my clothes. When I sent my friends in Ukraine pictures, they said, 'That's not you! That's not Oksana!' But when I call and talk with them, then they say, 'Oksana, you haven't changed so much. You still have the same voice, the same mind, the same everything.'" ❀

OPPOSITE PAGE AND THIS PAGE, TOP ROW, LEFT TO RIGHT: WITH HER FAVORITE DOLL AT AGE FIVE; BY TROY HOUSE. ABOVE, CLOCKWISE FROM TOP RIGHT: AT THE BEACH AT AGE FOUR; AT HOME RECENTLY WITH HER DOG, RUDIK, BY BETTY MARSHALL/SHOOTING STAR; WITH RUDIK BY BETTY MARSHALL/SHOOTING STAR; AT AGE THREE AND A HALF IN SKATES HER GRANDFATHER BOUGHT HER.

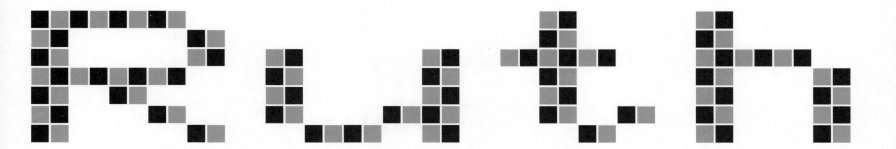

Ruth

Ruth Sheldon

Chess Player
16 years old
Born in Guilford,
lives in Manchester, England

The first time Ruth Sheldon ever set eyes on a chess set was New Year's Eve 1986. A family friend was visiting Ruth's family in Manchester, England, for the holidays. He had come bearing gifts, one of which was a wooden game set. Ruth was six, and she was fascinated with the rooks, ♞ knights, bishops, and queens ♛ way above the draughtsmen and backgammon pieces. "But it wasn't like I immediately said, 'I have to play this,'" she recalls. "I mean, I knew the moves, but I wasn't particularly interested."

By the time she hit 13, Ruth was the world under-14 girls champion. That, she says, "was amazing," but she had a hard time with all the praise and attention. "The papers were kind of saying, 'Ruth Sheldon, one of the best chess players in the world,' and all this kind of, like, chess genius stuff," she says quietly. "I mean, I really enjoy playing and I think I'm talented at chess, but I don't think I'm a prodigy."

Ruth went through a bit of disillusionment about – or, rather, disinterest with – the game. This period was between the ages of six and eight. Then, out of curiosity, she "kind of went along to the school chess club, and I got on the team, like, as the bottom player – the worst player, just the bottom." But she swiftly and steadily improved until she was beating all the other under-nine players. To this day, she feels she owes much of her success to the boys: "I used to get lots of comments from boys, like,

PHOTO COURTESY OF CHESHIRE LIFE

'Girls can't play chess,' and things like that. You know, girls are not really encouraged to play chess, that's what I've always found. There are a lot of people who argue that women don't have the kind of killer instinct you need, and that their minds aren't suited to it, and all this sort of thing – which is just complete rubbish." Yet she freely admits

through a phase where I started picking fights with my mom and dad. I'd claim that they weren't being good to me because I'd just lost – which wasn't true at all." That went on for a few years, and though Ruth says she's trying "to be a bit more mature about losing," there are plenty of times when she just wants to go off somewhere by her-

would I ever want to give this up?"

The most thrilling moment of her brief but illustrious career so far: at 14, facing off against former world champion Anatoly Karpov. "He was actually playing four people at once, and I was one of them," she says. "I was so nervous – I mean, it was really, really funny, because I just thought, I'm going to lose; I just

that the first few times a boy snickered at her, she blew it. "One time I just blundered really early on in the game because I was so upset, and it was like they'd proved their point. But I enjoy it now if people try to say something like that to me, because it just gets me more fired up. I use it to beat them."

Now she thrives on the feeling of competition that nearly swallowed her whole. "When I first started playing, and I'd lose, I went

self and cry. But when she's winning, she says, there's not a feeling like it in the world. "If I'm doing well, I try not to think about the result, because that makes me feel really nervous. But when I actually know I'm winning, I suddenly start thinking, 'Wow, I'm going to beat this person!' and I get a real rush. I love the competitiveness, I love the strategic side of it, and I love beating people. You can just get lost in the game. That's when I think, Why

don't want to seem stupid." Ruth actually drew, which basically means that neither of them won – it was a tie.

There are several reasons why Ruth, who's now 16, says she will never become a pro chess player. Chief among those reasons is the "chess scene." "Once you become involved in chess, there's like this whole kind of chess social world, and, like, the only people you end up mixing with are chess players."

On the other hand, she's been traveling to matches all over the world since she was 12 – without her parents – and has, she says, gotten a little crazy with the other kids. "I remember when I went to Germany, I went with a group of 17-year-olds, and that was the first time that I kind of went out and had something to drink and everything. It was very

she says, "all my friends thought I was a complete nerd, you know, with like the anorak and glasses. And when I've spoken to people, like newspapers, they've said, 'We expected you to be really studious and boring.'" But Ruth's not, really. She wants people to see her as a typical girl from Manchester who doesn't read much but who just read *Trainspotting* and

normally measure myself, because it depresses me") and especially her weight. "I used to feel very fat," she says. "I lost a lot of weight when I was about 11. I mean, it was never really serious; I never had an eating disorder, really. I don't think. But I used to be much more unhappy with myself." She pauses. "All the kind of role models that you see, when you watch films or whatever, have this kind of ideal figure, and it makes me angry. But it's been going on for so long – the actual fashion changes, but the principle is still the same. There's always a pressure to have a certain look."

Chess, she says, has helped her get over a poor self-image. "Now I've got something that makes me feel like I stand out," she says, "and that makes things a lot easier. I feel like I prove myself through chess, so there's not so much pressure on me. I mean, I don't think I'm beautiful, but I'm quite happy with the way I look." She pauses. "But I still try to be careful about what I eat. Sometimes I think it shouldn't matter. But it does." ❦

exciting," she says. "It was nothing serious, although, like, a year ago, I played in the British Chess Championship and stayed in a flat with nine people about my age, and nobody took the tournament seriously at all." After losing those matches, Ruth decided it might be a good idea to separate the partying from the chess.

"When I first started playing,"

thought it was brilliant; who doesn't really care for clothes, but does like to get her jeans and Levi's cords at the local second-hand store; who likes to go to clubs and shows and who's seen Oasis at least twice, but has "gone off them a little bit, because I listened to them a bit too much." She worries about things like her height (she's 5'4" – "I don't

Serena and Venus Williams

Tennis Players
15 and 16 years old
Born in Michigan and California,
live in Florida, U.S.A.

Serena and Venus Williams both started playing tennis at four years old, which became abundantly clear when we talked. Venus, 16, turned pro a couple of years ago (which basically means she competes for money and has a lucrative endorsement deal with Reebok). Serena, who's 15, is still an amateur – she competes but gets none of the attendant goodies. Venus and Serena live with their parents (their dad manages them, and their mom's a homemaker) and three older sisters in Palm Beach Gardens, Florida. For the Williams gals, life's a big bowl of cherries sans pits.

JANE: Serena, how did you get started playing tennis at age four?

SERENA: Well, my dad saw someone winning a lot of money at one time, and he hadn't made that in a whole year, so he decided he wanted his kids to be in tennis.

JANE: Were you guys into it at that age?

VENUS: I really don't remember. I suppose I thought it was fun.

JANE: When did it become clear that this was something you were going to do?

VENUS: When did it become clear?

JANE: Mmm-hmm.

VENUS: It never became clear that this was what I was going to do. My dad always told me I was going to be a professional tennis player, so it was my inspiration to become one.

SERENA: We lived in California, and we moved to Florida when I was almost 10 because they had better tennis programs and things of that nature.

JANE: Was that an easy move for you?

SERENA: I didn't really have any friends or anything, so I guess it wasn't hard.

JANE: So what's your schedule like now?

SERENA: Well, I go to school in the morning, I come home at about 1:00, practice till about 4:00 or 5:00.

JANE: And then what?

SERENA: Well, I'm with Jehovah's Witnesses – my whole family is – and I go to the Kingdom Hall and go to meetings.

JANE: How influential would you say religion is to you?

VENUS: Very. It's a guideway to your life. If, all of a sudden, things come up in the path that you're on, you can say, "No, I'm not going to do this," or "Yes, this is up to my standards," or "Yes, with my morals I can tolerate this."

SERENA: I do like singing in my extra time. I take guitar lessons on Thursday nights.

VENUS: I play guitar, and when I can, I go surfing. I could never imagine wasting time. Just not to do something with my time isn't going to help me in the future. Most kids I'm around, they really aren't like that. They go home and hang out. Or I guess that's what they do. But you can't lay around.

JANE: Would you say that you're a serious person, Venus?

VENUS: No. Because I laugh all the time. But when it comes to certain things, like school and tennis, I'm serious. I mean, I joke and play on the court, too. But not very much.

JANE: Do you guys get to go out much?

SERENA: Well, we always have a lot of time for fun. So yes, we always get to go out and do things with people.

ALL PHOTOGRAPHS IN THIS CHAPTER EXCEPT FOR CHILDHOOD SHOTS ARE BY ALESE AND MORTON PECHTER.

JANE: What do you do?

SERENA: Well, we usually go to the mall and hang out, or go to the movies.

VENUS: I'll, like, go to a lot of stores, buy lots of jewelry and clothes. I go to Macy's and Saks – actually, at Saks and Bloomingdale's, I don't like what I see. I like Dollhouse, but I don't like Calvin Klein or Gap. Or Bongo! Their jeans aren't long enough – I'm 6'1". Plus, they're tapered at the ankle. I don't wear that. It's too hard to get them off!

SERENA: Venus and I go to Wet Seal, which is just like retro clothing style for young teenagers or so. And Contempo Casuals – did you ever hear of that?

JANE: Oh, sure. I love Contempo Casuals.

SERENA: I like buying little overall dresses and shiny material skirts. I guess I like skirts more than shorts and pants. I don't really own any jean-short things or pants at all. I can't really fit in them. And I wear regular, casual Reebok shoes most of the time.

JANE: Is there anybody who's got a style you really admire?

SERENA: I'm not really into the pop culture world. Like, do you know Brandy's style? I couldn't say I like hers because I don't even know what she wears. But she has nice music.

JANE: Do you ever have bad days when you don't like the way you look?

SERENA: Well, yeah. There are some days when I look in the mirror and, like, I need something.

JANE: What do you mean?

SERENA: Like, I need a little moisture or something.

JANE: But what else goes through your mind?

SERENA: Well, I guess on bad days I just don't like the way my arms are. Sometimes I feel they're a little too big and bulky. But my mom's like, "You don't have big arms."

JANE: Do you ever find yourself comparing yourself with other people?

SERENA: No. Because I feel that I am just as good as them. Or even better.

VENUS: I would never say I was insecure. We have this saying, like, "We're always happy that we're tall." I always like the way I look. I like my eyelashes. They're very curly. My eyebrows are pretty bushy. My teeth aren't conventional; they're just kind of square. I never wanted caps over them. And my hair is a little across my shoulders. I have braids and put beads in them, and change the colors – sometimes green, sometimes blue. It depends how I feel. And I love my height.

SERENA: I have pretty high cheekbones, and I have nice-sized lips. I have a nice color for my skin – when I put makeup on, it doesn't look right on me. And I wear beads in my hair. Overall, I'm a pretty nice-looking person.

JANE: I wish more girls felt that way. Where do you think you get your self-esteem from?

SERENA: Well, I guess my mom and Venus. My mom always taught me to be strong and have a lot of self-esteem – and I usually do the things that Venus does.

JANE: Like what?

SERENA: I usually like to do everything she does.

JANE: Do you ever feel any sense of competition with your sister?

SERENA: No. Not at all.

JANE: Do you guys have, like, a really tight group of friends? Or do you have a best friend?

SERENA: Actually, I never really had friends. Because Venus was always around.

JANE: Do you guys date at all?

VENUS: No.

JANE: Are you allowed to date yet?

VENUS: No.

JANE: Do you guys ever get sick of each other?

SERENA: No, never.

JANE: Really?

SERENA: We never really argue. Maybe it's because we're so close in age, so we get along really fine, really well. [Sighs]

JANE: What's the matter?

SERENA: Nothing.

JANE: When was the last time you guys had a fight?

VENUS: Oh, let's see. The other day we were out on the court and Serena hit a ball real hard at me. I just told her that if she hits it that hard, I'm still going to hit it back. I'm not going to be scared. That was it. It wasn't even a fight, just an exchange of words. We don't get nasty and mean – it seems so natural for people to fight, but I don't see why. I guess people are violent by nature.

JANE: Do you find it hard at all to relate to people your age?

VENUS: No, I don't feel it's hard to relate. I feel that sometimes the things they do are really foolish.

JANE: Like . . . ?

VENUS: Like drugs, and like playing around, you know, in school, and not learning anything, just not doing their work and getting nasty to the dean. What else do they do? Talk back to their parents, and be rebellious. I think that's foolish. I would never do those types of things myself.

JANE: Do you ever feel – being pro at such a young age – that you're maybe missing something?

VENUS: No. I really don't. ✹

Top row, left to right: Venus in 1995; Serena and Venus in 1996; Serena in 1996. Second row, left to right: Venus in 1996; Venus at age 11; Serena in 1995; Serena and Venus with their dogs. Third row, left to right: Venus at 18 months; Venus at age 11; Venus and Serena sit one out; the Williams family at home (left to right): sisters Isha and Lyndrea, dad Richard and mom Oracene, and Venus and Serena. Bottom row, left to right: Serena in 1995; Venus at age 12.

Sharon Anyimi

High School Student
16 years old
Born and lives in New York, U.S.A.

Sharon's been nearly blind since birth. She's 16 years old now, and has spent most of her life in a New York private school for the blind and visually impaired, where she lives during the week. While home on weekends, she attends programs at the Lighthouse in New York City.

She is sitting next to me in a conference room in the Lighthouse. She's just had her picture taken for this book, a somewhat uncomfortable experience for her since the flash hurt her eyes (though she loved trying on the different clothes and striking poses).

Sharon stares straight ahead, and I can't tell whether this is because she's self-conscious about her eyes, which have an opaque look and tend to wander. I ask Sharon to tell me what she thinks makes her an interesting person. "The fact that . . . ," she begins tentatively. "Well, when it comes to music, I know so much about it – about the artists, because I'm interested in knowing what they're about. I like music a whole lot," she says. "If I were to do an album," she says, "it'd probably be a mixture of R&B and hip-hop." She tells me she loves Nas and Janet Jackson, Mary J. Blige, and En Vogue. "And I love giving props to [Puffy Combs's record label] Bad Boy! Every time I hear that stuff on the radio, I'm like, 'Yeah, I represent Bad Boy, you know what I'm sayin'?" Sharon is facing me and smiling broadly.

She goes on to tell me she is passionate about singing and performing. She first sang at a talent show at summer camp when she was seven, has performed in various other venues, and one day she'd even like to sing at the Apollo. She likes music class, and plays the drums. She likes to write poetry, and she keeps a journal. She's also been a cheerleader, and run track with sighted people (using thin ropes to indicate the division between lanes). She even spent last summer volunteering as an office aide at Bronx Lebanon Hospital. It seems clear that Sharon hasn't let her visual impairment stand in her way.

Who has taught me about beauty: My mother. She taught me to believe that beauty is both something that's on the surface and something that's within. How beautiful I am is how I feel.

Sharon starts playing with her hair, which is woven into thin, sleek braids. "I just got my hair braided last weekend, and it took about six hours," she reports. "I like them because I don't have to worry about fixing my hair every day." I ask her how she feels about her appearance on the whole, how much thought goes into it. "Well, looks aren't everything. I don't think about it too much. I'm 90% tomboy. I wear jeans and sweatshirts. I need to take care of my face more often."

When I ask her how she defines beauty, she says, "Well, beauty really comes from the inside. It comes from you. I guess for some girls, it's hard, because they've been through so many bad things in their whole life, and there wasn't one person who ever complimented them about anything. So it's like, one girl could have total confidence, but then there could be another girl who has a lack of confidence because the people that she knows in her life are feeding her negative vibes. So it's going to be hard to have as much self-esteem as the next person because of that." Which one is Sharon? "I guess," she says, "I was in an environment where people gave me a positive outlook on me."

CB

136

CB

SOMETHING I INHERITED I WISH I HADN'T: MY DRY LIPS AND BIG THIGHS.

I wash my hair: Once a week. I wash my hair in braids and dry it naturally.

SOMETHING I INHERITED AND I LOVE: MY HEAD.

My deep, dark beauty secret: I never wash my face without my Dove liquid moisturizer.

I ask her how much she worries about her appearance. "Well, I do think about it," she says. She pauses. "If I'm going out in public, my hair isn't going to be all messed up and my face isn't going to be dirty. Because then everybody's looking at me, like, 'What happened to her?' You want to look good for the public.' When she does go out, she likes to wear dresses and skirts. She also wears makeup occasionally. She doesn't have much more to say on the subject.

Sharon does, however, talk very openly about how much she hates living in a dorm at school. "I can't bear it," she says. "Just being at the dorm, with all its rules . . . I just want to go home at the end of the day like everybody else." When she does go home on weekends and holidays, she loves not having to adhere to a strict schedule like at school. Still, her parents are protective. She doesn't get to go to as many parties as she wants, since she's not fully independent yet and they don't like her to travel great distances alone. However, she continues, "Slowly but surely it's progressing. I just wish I could, you know, go out to a party and have fun. I like hanging out with people. I love parties. I guess I'm somewhat jealous of my older brother and sister. They got to go anywhere they wanted. Sometimes I think it's my vision, that it makes my parents more protective. But

that's just how it is, you know?"

Sharon can attend school-sponsored formals. She doesn't mind getting dressed up for them, but doesn't seem terribly excited about it either, though she is interested in clothes. "I hear about these things," she says softly, "like Versace, and I can't help but wonder: What does that look like? Because I know there's something about it that catches people and makes them want to wear it."

As much as she longs just to be with other kids and go to parties and games and date boys and stuff, Sharon is wary of the way people – kids and adults – who don't understand what it's like to be visually impaired might act. When asked whether she'd ever like to go to regular public school, she says she thinks her vision would have to be better to be able to do that, because those schools are still not equipped to accommodate children with special needs like large-type books. "If my vision wasn't the way it is . . . I get angry because my vision gets in the way of things. It's hard for me to read textbooks. Because that's what teachers would do, they'd throw me this textbook and say, 'Read this,' and I'd be like, 'I can't read this; this is small.' And I would have trouble with the fact that, you know, there are other kids and teachers acting ignorant and stupid because they have some comment about students who are visually impaired or non-

sighted. I mean, I know it's not my fault that I came out this way. It's just . . . how it is."

Sharon picks up a couple of her Polaroids (from the shoot) on the table; she holds them less than an inch from her eyes and studies them intently. She's smiling to herself. I ask her what she thinks of them, what she thinks of herself – does she think that she's a pretty girl? "Yeah," she says, without missing a beat. I tell her that she's the first person I've talked to who has said yes without a moment's hesitation. "Really?" she says, turning to me. "Cool." And she takes another look at herself. ✤

AT AGE EIGHT ON A TRIP TO GHANA

I FEEL THE MOST BEAUTIFUL WHEN: I AM ABLE TO MAKE OTHERS HAPPY OR MAKE A DIFFERENCE.

My biggest as-yet-unanswered beauty question: How would it be possible to keep my lips moist at all times without putting Chapstick on frequently?

Summer Phoenix

Actress
18 years old
Born in California,
lives in Florida, U.S.A.

At 18, Summer Phoenix has lived in Argentina, Mexico, Los Angeles, Florida, and New York. She's traveled to Australia and Costa Rica, and to Ecuador with some "eco-warrior" friends of her mom's, and she's acted in a couple of movies, although she says she'd like to consider the one she just finished, *Arresting Gina*, her first. "That was pretty ace," she says. Also, she's a brand-new aunt.

"It was amazing," says Summer, who was with her sister, Liberty, when she gave birth at her family's home in Florida. "She had the baby in water – it's more soothing for the mother. And the baby lives in water for the first nine months, so it was an amazing, simple transition for him. He came out eyes open under the water. So cute. I was crying the entire time, but Liberty didn't cry once. She didn't even take an Advil for the pain." They named the baby Rio, which is Spanish for River.

A huge chunk of Summer's otherwise nomadic childhood was spent in Florida, where she attended a progressive school. "It was totally chill," she says. "There were only 23 kids for four different grades, and we had different animals – peacocks, lambs, dogs. We didn't start till 10:00 in the morning, and we had, like, a morning meeting where we 'shared stuff.' I loved it." When she finished up there, Summer decided to get her GED rather than go to public school. "I couldn't have dealt," she says. "I mean, I'm different, and a lot of kids like to pick on that, you know? Like, 'Ooh, you're gross! What

are you eating? Tofu salad?!' And I knew I would get that kind of s— there." After she got her diploma, Summer did a semester of film school at NYU – "and that's been the end of my education so far." But she thinks she wants to continue acting. "It was always something I did when I was younger," she says. "I mean, my whole family did it, and I totally enjoyed it and loved it. I did a lot of TV – one really bad cheesy movie. Then I moved away to Central America, and I totally didn't think about it. But when I came back to America, I started to think, Oh, what am I going to do with my life?"

Summer knows that some people see her as something of a hippie chick, and she pokes fun at this image

constantly. She picked our meeting place because it's vegan, which means it serves no meat and no dairy. Yet when I showed up, she was lounging at an outdoor table, smoking a cigarette. "I know!" she exclaims. "Such a sham!" She laughs. "Me and my older sister were picking butts off the ground and stuff when I was about 14. I've been smoking way too long. But," she adds unapologetically, "there's nothing better than coffee and a cigarette."

And though you'd probably picture her in crunchy, earth-toned, flowing hippie outfits, her style's much more complex: today she's wearing a fitted, kind of demure light-floral print dress with an excellent tailored navy blue coat and an old-school white fuzzy hat ringed with a band of fake diamonds – all thrift-store finds. "I do wear pretty much all secondhand junk," she says. "There are tons of old people that die – estate sales and stuff like that. Then there's tons of people that just don't know how cool their s—❀ is, so they just give it to the Salvation Army. And I'm, like, there."

Her personal style, she says, is called "stugly. It's just like finding the ugliest

piece of clothing you can and then just taking a step back, breathing, taking all the colors in, and just going, 'Yeah, that could look good,'" she explains. "I think I'm a bit eclectic, and I'm just so not into everybody wearing the same thing. I like to wear lots of different things all together. I like wearing tights and socks and leg warmers," she says. She looks serious, and I have no reason not to believe her. As for makeup, she says she never wears it. "But I always wear glitter," she explains. "It's

just always been my thing – I don't know why." She closes her eyelids so I can see the light dusting of white she's sprinkled on her lashes. "I mean, makeup was never in the house. My mom doesn't wear makeup, she doesn't wear jewelry, she doesn't shave her legs. So the sun was always my makeup – I'm that skin tone that never gets pale. And I have dark eyelashes and dark eyebrows, so I never needed mascara, or to pencil in my

eyebrows. I've always felt uncomfortable in makeup, like, 'God, it's runny' or something – it just makes me feel self-conscious. Glitter is different, because it can go anywhere. Get it in my hair, get in on my cheeks, it's fine."

We finish our lunch, so Summer and I walk a few blocks to Porto Rico, her favorite coffee shop. She loves it because it's dark and smoky and the air is thick with a coffee-bean smell. She sits down and pulls a small

I FELT THE LEAST BEAUTIFUL: YESTERDAY.

I FEEL THE MOST BEAUTIFUL: RIGHT NOW.

MY DEEP, DARK BEAUTY SECRET: A SIMPLE MANTRA WORKS BEST:
SOMETHING LIKE "GENIUS AND BEAUTY". REPEAT 100 TIMES.

OPPOSITE PAGE: TREES SAVED BY ECO-RICA IN THE OSA PENINSULA IN COSTA RICA, 1996. INSET: SUMMER AT AGE SEVEN.

cardboard container of soy milk out of her purse as I stir whole cow's milk into my cup. "Does regular milk taste good?" she asks. I tell her yeah, and she squirts the soy milk out of the container and all over her dress. "Oh s—!" she says, laughing. "I do this all the time."

Summer's got a flight to catch ✈ in a couple of hours – one of her best friends is getting married in London. "I just bought the dress I'm going to wear for $1.75," she says proudly. "But I had to get it altered because it had a stain on the neck, and it was really obvious, so I just had it cut and pulled in." And though Summer conforms for no one, she's a little concerned about how her unshaven pits will go over at the reception. "My friend, the one who's getting married, her father is Pakistani," she says, "and his side is all conservative and proper. And England is just very, you know, steeped in whatever. I was thinking, Wow, I'm wearing a sleeveless dress, God, I wonder if these people are going to be totally bothered by my armpit hair." So she figures she'll wear a shawl. But otherwise, she couldn't care less what other people have to say. 👊"Guys have come up to me," she says, "and they're like, 'If I gave you a shaver, would you shave your armpits?' And I'm like, 'If I gave you a hammer, would you smash your f—in' face in?'"

The only time she does give serious thought to the way she looks is when she goes on auditions – but that doesn't mean she acts on those thoughts. "I feel like when my attitude is great and positive," she says, "it doesn't matter what I look like. At least not to me. I mean, I totally walked into this one audition with huge pants on and my hair up, ✎ which my agent tells me" – she puts on a New York accent – "NEVAH WEAH YAH HAYEH UP!" She cackles. "I don't know – I guess I'm more *sultry* looking when it's down. But I was just bubbly and great, and I think it was because of that. It was obviously not my looks, because I was totally skanked out." So she's pretty pleased with herself, even though

she doesn't know if she's gotten the part.

When she was pretty young she noticed physical traits she shares with her brothers and sisters. "Like, me and my sisters are *built*," she says. "No matter how much I did drugs, I would never be skinny. But I remember just looking at my oldest sister's friends and my brothers' girlfriends, and just being like, 'Yo, they're a lot different. They're really skinny.'" Then there was the time when she and her family were living in South America and she shaved all her hair

Beauty product I'd love to forget: All makeup except glitter.

IF YOU GAVE ME $100 TO SPEND ON BEAUTY EXCITEMENT, I'D BUY: GLITTER.

I CAN'T LIVE WITHOUT MY: GLITTER.

SUMMER JOY PHOENIX

I wash my hair: Once a week I wash it but I rinse every other day.

HOW LONG IT TAKES ME TO GET READY FOR SCHOOL: I QUIT SCHOOL AT 15 AFTER GRADUATING. REMEMBER "GENIUS AND BEAUTY" 100 TIMES.

THE BEST BEAUTY TRICK I'VE LEARNED: DON'T.

BACKGROUND PHOTO ON BOTH PAGES: THE ANDES FOREST, IN ECUADOR. INSET, THIS PAGE: SUMMER WITH THE MAYOR OF QUITO IN 1996. INSETS, OPPOSITE PAGE, CLOCKWISE FROM TOP: WITH HER MOM IN COSTA RICA, 1996; AT AGE THREE; WITH HER AUSTRALIAN FRIENDS IN ECUADOR, 1996.

off, only to come down with a staph infection. "It's like, an itty little sore gets, like, big and puss-y. I got it from the water, and it was just all over my face and my legs, and inside my nose – I mean, it was pretty tragic. Because there are a lot of babes in Argentina."

I ask Summer if she considers herself pretty, and she says she can't say it. "I think that when one looks in the mirror," she begins carefully, "you see what you don't like, you don't see what you like. I can never look in the mirror and see my face. I always go, 'Oh, my eyebrows are really bushy, and my nose is way too long.' But," she says, "I'm pretty comfortable with myself. I know that I have a lot better of a time when I am, and that is always pending on my mind whenever I start to get down on myself about my physical appearance. Because it feels s—ty – if you think you're too fat, how can you go to the beach and have a blast with your friends? It's just not worth it. So not worth it. It's a total waste, especially of youth. Time goes by way too fast to take much time feeling s—ty." She stubs out her cigarette.

"It's a fine line," she continues. "There have been times when I was crying until I couldn't anymore, where it's just complete grief and at the lowest low. I would've traded *anything* not to feel that emptiness and that void. And that emptiness and that void is just complete neglect of yourself and your soul." She pauses and eyes the action at the counter. "I went from boyfriend to boyfriend – I had doting boyfriends, I had boyfriends that

I've been involved in environmental issues since I was pretty young. I have particularly been connected to YES (Youth for Environmental Sanity) out of Santa Cruz, California. They have summer camps where the youth from all over come and experience nature as well as are educated about what has been happening on the Earth. They also tour high schools, bringing the celebration of the beauty of life and what kids can do to sustain it.

My own personal pet project is Eco-Rica Preservation, a non-profit organization that my family and a good friend started several years ago. Its primary purpose is to purchase land that is threatened and protect it in its natural state. It's very exciting and fulfilling. Our first purchase in Costa Rica was actually buying logging rights back from the loggers just before they were about to cut down the trees.

SOMETHING I INHERITED I WISH I HADN'T: SOCIETALLY IMPOSED NEUROSES.

didn't pay me much attention – one extreme to the other. And I always felt like I was alone, no matter whether I was with somebody or not. I could feel ugly if I looked fine or if they were telling me I was beautiful. Then, finally, when I took the time out to try and start to love myself, which is such an intense, hard process, that's when I . . ." she trails off.

Summer checks her watch and suggests that we get going; she's got a wedding gift to buy before she catches her flight. We grab our coats and head out onto the street. But before she goes, she thinks of one other thing she wants to tell me. "The one thing I learned is that you have to do it for yourself," says Summer. "I think it's been proven

so many times that beauty comes from the inside – that you have to realize it for yourself, exude that and be that. Otherwise it doesn't make the same impact on you or your soul or your ability to shine." She cracks a wide smile. "You're as beautiful as you feel," she says. "To quote Carole King."

MY FAVORITE HOMEMADE BEAUTY CONCOCTION: RESCUE REMEDY FROM NEALS YARD (LONDON).

SOMETHING I INHERITED AND LOVE: MY FAMILY.

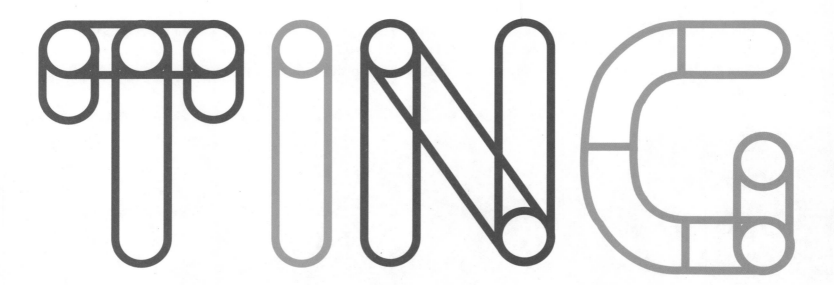

When she was a little girl growing up in Shanghai, Ting Luo's dad never read her fairy tales or stories from children's books. "He used to bring me around, you know, to science museums," she says. "We would go to the harbor and we would take the ferry for the whole day. And we would talk about different things; you know, the water flow, how the boat is going this way, that way – just different things. I mean, that's when I was really, really, really little. And, like, as opposed to saying, 'Oh, that's interesting,' I was supposed to know how it works and why it works and is there some way we can improve it." Last year, 18-year-old Ting won a Westinghouse science award, worth $40,000, for investigating gene expression.

Ting's father was a professor at a university in China. Her mother was an accountant. By the time she was 13, she had shown such promise that her parents decided that they should emigrate to America. "Basically, my parents believed that college education is, like, a lot better here as opposed to China," she says. "They thought I should go to high school here, so I could get used to the language, the customs, so that I could go to college here." But Ting wasn't down with it. "I said, 'No, I don't need to go to the United States, I'm fine in China,'" she recalls. "But my parents convinced me that, you know, education is more important for my future." (Her mother now works in the home, while her father teaches at a local junior high.)

Ting enrolled in Stuyvesant High School in New York City, one of the most academically rigorous public schools in the country. And though she had been taught basic English as a kid in China – "you learn A-B-C-D," she says – she picked up most of it through American television. And while she says she didn't experience much culture shock, there were a couple of things that surprised her. "I find that here, the teacher doesn't really know the students as well," she says. "It's less personal. They come in, they teach, and then they just leave, as opposed to when I was in China, my teachers and I, we'd actually hang out. We'd talk and do things together after school." And there's more pressure in China to excel. "You know how Chinese, they like to save face, whatever?" she asks. "Parents talk with their friends, 'Oh, where does your daughter go to school? What kind of grades does she get?' So it's not really for the sake of the child sometimes. It's really for parents themselves to look good, to sound good. And all my old friends, I know that they go to prep schools and now they have special tutors and whatever. Every day they work until midnight. It's kind of sad."

Ting herself has always been a big believer in self-motivation. "It's all really dependent on you, that you

ABOVE: HARD AT WORK IN CHINA AT AGE NINE. BELOW: AT AGE 10 WITH HER DAD IN CHINA.

have to go for yourself," she says. "I know that my parents always tried to educate me just to be very observant and think about what's going on – because if I were to grow up according to standard Chinese society, I would just be, you know, reading a book all day, trying to work out some weird math equation, just sitting there and memorizing." And her parents' method helped her immensely by the time she got to New York. "In a place like Stuyvesant," she says, "there are so many bright kids, really, really bright kids. And not just in academia, but kids really just excel in a lot of different subjects and different areas. So you really have to be self-motivated and self-driven, I guess, to do well."

Winning the Westinghouse award, she says, was totally overwhelming. "Now, to think back, I say, 'Wow, how did I ever really pull it off?'" she says with a laugh. "It was really a lot of work. Initially, it was, I guess, tough, because the subject itself is very deep. There was so much background research and background reading I had to do that, in a way, is very boring. But it gets

interesting once you know what's going on, and during this whole experiment, the more I did it, the more interesting it became. Because you can feel it. And, like, I actually feel proud, I think."

Ting is in love with science because, she says, "it expands your brain. You actually understand how we are the way we are. Science, in a way, is unpredictable. It's, like, mysterious. In a way, that's really beautiful. Like, for biology, I get these really pretty data, and I call them 'beauty,' because they're so hard to argue."

Though she pays no mind to makeup or hair or fashion ("I just wear what's comfortable as opposed to buying the brand name here nowadays for teenagers"), Ting became aware of what it means to be physically beautiful at a very young age. "When I was little," she says, "no one ever told me, 'Ting, you're pretty.' The common compliments I received actually were more like, 'Oh, Ting, you're such a smart girl,' 'Oh, Ting, you're so well behaved,' 'Oh, Ting, that's such a pretty dress.' Even nowadays, I talk about it with my parents, but it's only a joke. I say, 'Mom, I never received any pretty compliments – it's always I'm smart, or I have good grades, I do well, I know this, I know that. Mom, why is that? Huh?'" Ting takes a breath. I think maybe she's going to laugh, but she doesn't.

She looks, she says, like an intellectual. "You can have the typical nerdy kind of look," she says tentatively. "And there's also the more slick, smart kind of look." And which look is hers? "I don't know," Ting answers. "I really look very neat, very clean. I like a simple-cut suit." Her tone brightens. "For Westinghouse," she says, "the girls are supposed to wear a suit, so I actually had to go out to some upscale stores and buy some, I guess, dressed-up stuff – business-looking. And I liked it! I like that kind of clothing. So nowadays," she says conspiratorially, "I'll even buy them."

1. "If you walk down the street in China, you see all these, I guess around 20-ish people, they're all in really rather formal dresses, dresses you would wear to a semiformal of some sort. And, you know, they wear them to the workplace. And here, I think, people my age at least, the majority tend to dress down – they wear jeans and T-shirts."

2. "In China, if you're a middle-aged woman, you're not supposed to wear some bright red skirt, or you're not supposed to wear a short skirt – period. You're not supposed to wear anything that's very young looking, something that a 25- or 30-year-old might wear if you're 50. As opposed to here, I see middle-aged women wearing pretty clothes – they look young, they feel good. But in China you're supposed to dress according to your age group."

3. "Everything is more explicit here. You have so many fashion magazines. There are so many things going on about fashion, about looks and makeup. Back there, I don't think it's as dominant. Here everything is more extreme. But even where you have more freedom to do whatever, like this is a free country and so forth, there's even more pressure to conform and to look a certain way."

Right now, Ting's a freshman at the Massachusetts Institute of Technology in Cambridge, where she lives in an all-female dorm. It's there, she says, where she really feels the tyranny of a set standard. "There are so many American girls that place such a stress on how they look," she says incredulously. "Even my friends, they're always like, 'I'm on a diet, I'm on a diet.' And I'm like, 'Stupid.' If you're on a diet, you're not eating enough or you're not eating well. You get dizzy. You can't concentrate in class. Your grades go down. I mean, it's a really bad cycle. You know," she adds proudly, "I eat like a pig.

"And I never really wonder if I'm pretty or not," she goes on. "I really think that if people like me, they should like me for who I am, for, I guess, my thoughts – just my personality, as opposed to, 'Oh, you look cute' or 'Oh, you look ugly.' You know, when I wear a

THIS PAGE, CLOCKWISE, STARTING FROM TOP RIGHT: AT THE PIANO AT AGE 10; ACCEPTING THE WESTINGHOUSE AWARD IN NEW YORK CITY IN 1996; PRIMPING AT AGE FOUR; AS A SENIOR AT STUYVESANT HIGH SCHOOL IN NEW YORK CITY IN 1995, WHEN SHE SPENT EVERY SPARE MOMENT WORKING ON HER WESTINGHOUSE PROJECT; AT AGE FOUR WITH HER AUNT, DAD, AND MOM IN SHANGHAI; BY CB; AT AGE THREE, AT THE "LONG WIND" PARK IN SHANGHAI; BY CB; AT AGE THREE IN THE "LONG WIND" PARK; BY CB; BY CB.

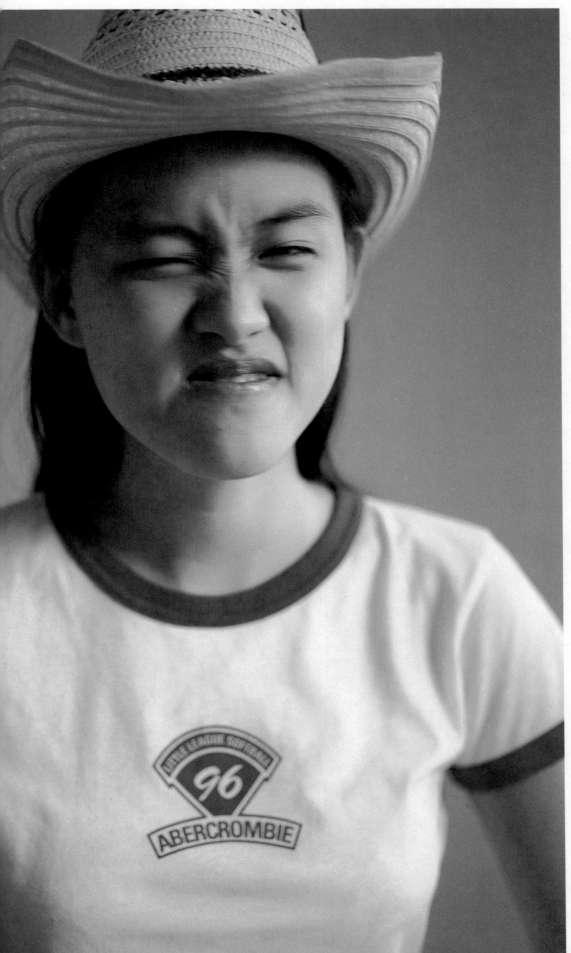

pretty dress and people compliment me, I'm happy. I'm like, 'Okay, thank you.' But . . . I don't know. I just really don't care anymore."

Maybe Ting's so cool with the way she looks because her parents never told her that it was a measure of her value; maybe it's because she's a genius, and she's got genetic codes to crack; maybe it's because she never really thought she was a stunner to begin with and just made her peace with that idea. She herself can't pinpoint why she's so cool with herself – but then she tells a story that seems to explain it. "The other day," she says, "my father was taking a plane some- where, and he started talking to the person sitting next to him. He was showing my dad his family, his pic- tures, so my dad showed my family, my pictures. And the man took a look at my picture and said, 'Well, let me first compliment you not on whether your daughter looks good or not – what I really want to tell you is that your daughter looks very, very confident.' Even in a pic- ture," she says, "the topic of how confident I was just came up, and my dad told me that, and I'm like, 'Wow.' I mean, that's an indication of how I am."

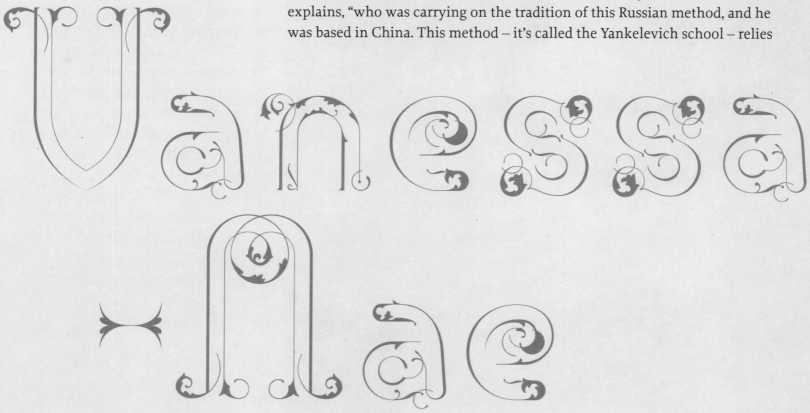

BY SARAH MAINGOT

"I mean, one person called me a 'Lolita,'" says 17-year-old violinist Vanessa-Mae. She's telling me about the initial, violent reaction to her first-ever pop CD cover, which depicted her – at 15 – hip-deep in the ocean, clad in a damp, white sundress, violin tucked under her chin. "It was astonishing! I probably wouldn't bother analyzing these people's minds, because I think a lot of them were very, very sick people. And being a normal 15-year-old, I didn't even think about, Are people going to like this? Are people going to find it attractive? I just thought about it for myself, and I thought, Well, I like that. I am somebody who was born in a hot country. I am used to being in the sea. I was a water baby from a very young age. I am comfortable in water. I have a connection with water anyway. When other kids go on holiday," she continues, "and they take pictures of each other on horseback or water-skiing or snow skiing, they put it in a frame in their bedroom. That was the same for me. It was just that instead of putting it in a frame in my bedroom, I put it on a CD cover for the world to see."

Vanessa-Mae was born in Singapore. Her parents divorced when she was a baby. When her mother, then a lawyer, married the guy she calls her "second father," who's English and also a lawyer, she and her mother moved to London. In kindergarten, she got into plunking away at the piano, but got frustrated because her feet couldn't reach the pedals. So she picked up the violin instead. "I mean, at that point it wasn't anything special," says Vanessa-Mae. "But even though I wasn't taking it seriously, teachers would come to my parents and say, 'She's got promise and potential. It would be a shame not to get her into music.' So I did start taking a few more lessons a week, and then I started to get more passionate about music."

By the time she was eight, she says, she knew the violin was her life. At the urging of her teachers, she and her mother went off to China so Vanessa-Mae could study violin intensively. "There was basically one teacher," she explains, "who was carrying on the tradition of this Russian method, and he was based in China. This method – it's called the Yankelevich school – relies

Vanessa-Mae

Violinist
17 years old
Born in Singapore
Lives in London, England

MY FAVORITE HOMEMADE BEAUTY CONCOCTION: A MILK BATH - NOT
DONKEY'S MILK, JUST GOOD-QUALITY FULL-CREAM MILK.

MY BIGGEST AS-YET-UNANSWERED BEAUTY QUESTION: WHY BEAUTY IS SO INDIVIDUAL?

on the fact that playing the violin has got to be second nature to you. It was all quite daunting for an eight-year-old, but I was a tough little cookie." By this point, her mother had already quit law to devote herself full-time to Vanessa-Mae and her burgeoning talent. Six months later, they returned to London. Vanessa-Mae then applied to the Senior College of Music; she's the youngest person ever accepted. By the time she was 12, she had cut her first record and embarked on a tour.

She still has a bit of high school left to complete, but she works with private tutors in between recording, shooting videos, and touring, and she wouldn't have it any other way. "For me, this is a natural life," she says. "I never missed out on a childhood, because I had it. You have a childhood, and it's what you do with it that matters. Now, I had my fair share of birthday parties and tea parties, but I knew when I started taking music seriously . . ." She sighs. "Nobody said it was going to be easy-teasy."

Vanessa-Mae seems to thrive on challenge. The first time we spoke, she was in the middle of choosing cover shots for her new CD. The second time, she called me from Poland, where she was in the ninth month of a world tour. Actually, she told me touring is one of her absolute favorite things, and she orchestrates every single element of her shows, down to the appropriate costumes and makeup. "You know," she says, "I see myself when I'm playing in a live concert as an all-around entertainer. When people play an album on their CD player, they don't care what I look like, but when they come to see me play, I think they're looking at the whole spectacle." Depending on the style of music she's playing – classical, pop, or rock-based stuff – Vanessa-Mae dresses herself accordingly, but always in clothes that will allow her to move freely.

"Like, last night was a classical concert, so I wore three ball dresses," she says. "But on my kind of pop tour, there I am in biking shorts under a short dress with Doc Martens, because when I'm working with dancers, I've got to be, you know, in sensible shoes." Among her favorite designers are Issey Miyake, Dolce & Gabbana, and Versace, who designed one of her favorite costumes: a black chain metal dress, which is so heavy she can only wear it for about an hour at a time. And she is a huge fan of natural fibers, which are key when she's playing furiously under hot lights.

She describes her style as "eclectic," and when she's not performing, Vanessa-Mae likes wearing beat-up Levi's, crop-topped tees, and "stomping around in chunky boots." But for the most part, what she wears is always meant to enhance the music. "It all depends on my mood, the project that I'm working on, and the environment in which I'm performing," she says. "Like, in my first pop videos, it was funky clothes like crop-tops and hot pants and biker boots." That's an understatement. In her video for a piece she calls "Toccata and Fugue," Vanessa-Mae uses her various outfits to illustrate the way she likes to juxtapose classical works with modern music: she's seen in, alternately, a long, simple black dress; a citron-y, girlish one about half that length; purple shorts paired with a black lycra midriff top and knee-high biker boots; and the aforementioned white sundress. "Like my music," she says, "it's a fusion of varied styles."

Makeup, she says, is strictly for performing. "I started wearing it when I turned professional," says Vanessa-Mae, "so I guess I was about 11 years old. But not heavy makeup – no 11-year-old can wear heavy makeup. Just to control shine and stuff on TV or on a

I felt the least beautiful when: I remember being at the top of a fantastic glacier called Diavolezza in St. Moritz. The beauty of my natural surroundings was so overwhelming that I felt minuscule, trivial, and frankly un-beautiful in the midst of all that splendor.

WHO HAS TAUGHT ME ABOUT BEAUTY: ANYONE WHO IS BEAUTIFUL IN BODY AND/OR MIND AROUND ME.

My deep, dark beauty secret: Think about good, happy, beautiful things.

Beauty product I'd love to forget: Hair spray.

I FELT THE MOST BEAUTIFUL: WHEN I PERFORMED IN FRONT OF 200,000 PEOPLE AT THE G7 CONCERT IN FRANCE. THE LIGHTING FELT WONDERFUL AND THE FIREWORKS SHOW AROUND ME GAVE ME A GLOW WHICH ENHANCED MY FEEL-GOOD FACTOR.

I FREAK OUT IF I LEAVE HOME WITHOUT MY: SUNGLASSES.

IF YOU GAVE ME $100 TO SPEND ON BEAUTY EXCITEMENT, I'D BUY: WHATEVER MY MAKEUP ARTIST SAYS IS MISSING OR GETTING LOW IN MY KIT.

concert stage." If she's on a long tour, she travels with a makeup artist, whose one bit of advice is to get enough sleep. (Right now, she's getting by on about four hours a night, even though she needs seven.) "One of the weirdest things that I find hard to come to terms with – because it's still so distressing – is the *diktat* not to wash your hair too often," she says in all seriousness. Why? "Because then it gets too difficult to style," Vanessa-Mae tells me. "But I prefer not to wear makeup. I mean, it gives your skin a chance to breathe. Just put on a pair of sunglasses and you'll always look fresh."

Although Vanessa-Mae's done fashion shoots for British magazines like *Tatler* and was once chosen as one of *People* magazine's "50 Most Beautiful," she says that she wouldn't call herself pretty. "I guess if somebody else says that, then it's a compliment," she reasons. "But it's kind of arrogant to say that you're pretty." Besides, she says, "beauty" is a word that's often used too literally and is too often associated with the style of the moment. "I think that basically, if someone is attractive, they can't help it," Vanessa-Mae says. "It's not like a dress you can put on. It's either something that you have or you don't. You can put two people in the same dress, the same clothes, but one is more attractive than the other. Beauty has so much to do with the soul of a person – the way they hold themselves, the way they act, the way they move, what kind of person they are deep down."

As for herself, she would prefer to be defined by her music. "First of all, when I was a kid, one of the things that really attracted me to the violin was its physical attributes," she says. "When you run your hand over it, it's almost like a human body. It's a very physical instrument – you tuck it under your chin, next to your skin. It's almost like cuddling a pet or a doll. It's such a compact and beautiful instrument. There is a distinction, for me, between pop and classical music." And the way she feels when she plays, she says, is unlike anything else. "I draw this analogy, when playing classical music," Vanessa-Mae says, "that it's like the Mona Lisa. I am not creating anything new. Obviously, every night I play differently, but that's not technically creating a new sound. Every night I am like the light that shines on it. I could be blue, I could be green, I could be a different ray, a different heat, a different intensity – but I am the light." ❁

Something I inherited I wish I hadn't: Baby hair.

I WASH MY HAIR: ONCE EVERY TWO DAYS AS LONG AS IT IS NOT JUST BEFORE A TV SHOW OR A PHOTO SHOOT.

I can't live without my: Oral-B toothbrush (size 35, indicator right-angled, blue) and Colgate Total toothpaste, Pears cleansing bar, Witch Hazel (any brand).

OPPOSITE PAGE, TOP: ST. MORITZ, A PLACE VANESSA-MAE FINDS BEAUTIFUL; BOTTOM, LEFT, BY PETER HUMMEL/REPORT H+H; RIGHT, IN FRONT OF THE DRESDEN OPERA HOUSE, BY JOHN PAUL. THIS PAGE, TOP: HER DOG, KIM-SUNG; BOTTOM: BY MIKE OWEN.

JANE PRATT THANKS:
Dan Strone
Maureen Callahan
Brad Johns
Chris Cusano
Christan Burran
Christy Bush
Mary Clarke
Liz Brous
Richard Hofstetter
Frank Messa
Trinity, John
Seth Flicker
Sheila Blake/Mom
Vernon Pratt/Dad
Peter
Amy
Dan
Hill
Ben
Debi
Sarina
G&G
Lily
Caroline
Rosie
Jake
Gaby
Tommy

CALLAWAY WISHES TO SINCERELY THANK:
Christy Bush, master portraitist, who hung with these girls and captured their characters and beauty on film. Christy, your spirit, good nature, and enthusiasm were a constant support.

Christan Burran, inspired makeup artist, who worked closely and carefully with us to come up with the ultimate beauty tips for young women.

Patrik Andersson
Lydia Anyimi
Eika Aoshima
Dallas Austin
Barbara Bergeron
Dave Black
L.T. Bramble
Richard Brooks
Liz Brous
Kelly Bush
Mara Buxbaum
Michael Carlisle
Nancy Carson
Bob Carlos Clarke
Eric Connolly
Chris Cusano
Dance Theatre of Harlem
Melinda Dancil
Keven Davis
Gerald Drucker
Daniela Federici
Stan Feig
Karen Folland
Sandy Friedman
Ramona Godfrey
Nicolai Grosell
Caroline Grunwald
Randy Haecker
Sarah Hall
Midori Harada
Brian Hatch
Hetrick-Martin Institute
Quinn Hood
The HoriPro Agency
Troy House
Peter Hummel
Brad Johns
Sam Jones
Jorge
Minette Joyce
Damir Keretic

Jerry Kirsch
Kelly Klein
Anne Korando of Science Service, Inc.
Wooten Lee
Leslie Lopez
Bei Bei Shen and Heming Luo
Sarah Maingot
Sachi Maki
Didier Malige
Betty Marshall
Stacie Middleton
Camelia and Dimitry Moceanu
Melanie Molitor
David Newell
Frank Ockenfels
Linda Omichinski
Mike Owen
James Leslie Parker
Jennifer Karen Parr
Nigel Parry
John Paul
Alese and Morton Pechter
Daniel Peebles
Everett Perry
Heart Phoenix
L. L. Pomeroy
Natalie Portman's parents
Neal Preston
Teresa Ramsay
Paul Rubè
Diana Sares
Nico Schweizer
David Seidner
Sukanya Shankar
Paul Sinclaire
Ashley Smith
Matthew Jordan Smith
Francesca Sorrenti
Friederike von Stackelberg
Joyce Vordenbaum
Lyle Walker
Elizabeth and Albert Watson
Cliff Watts
Whitney Wildman
Oracene and Richard Williams
Vernice Williams
Calvin Wilson
Cornel Windlin
Firooz Zahedi
Ellen Zeisler

CHRISTY BUSH THANKS:
Ron Egozi, Mark Williams, Kip Bogdahn,
Jimmy Morris, Elena Columbo, Jon Mintz,
Sam Kretschmer, Steven Alan, Jane Pratt,
Everyone at The Color Resource Center,
and Breezy Shores #7.

OPPOSITE PAGE, TOP: NICHOLAS CALLAWAY IN HIGH SCHOOL. SECOND ROW, LEFT TO RIGHT: JENNIFER WAGNER AT HER EIGTH GRADE GRADUATION IN WYCKOFF, NEW JERSEY; ALEXANDRA ARROWSMITH WITH HER BEST FRIEND ALISON AT AGE 17 IN NEW YORK; ANTOINETTE WHITE AT AGE 17 IN ENGLAND (PHOTO BY NICHOLAS WHITE); CHRISTY BUSH IN HIGH SCHOOL IN MARIETTA, GEORGIA. THIRD ROW, LEFT TO RIGHT: TRUE SIMS IN PORTLAND, OREGON AT AGE 18; MONICA MORAN IN HIGH SCHOOL; PAULA LITZKY AT AGE 14. BOTTOM ROW, LEFT TO RIGHT: CHRIS STEIGHNER IN HIGH SCHOOL IN NORTH CAROLINA; RAOUL GOFF AT AGE 15 IN CALIFORNIA; IVAN WONG, JR. IN HIGH SCHOOL. SEE FOLLOWING PAGE FOR CREDITS.

BEYOND BEAUTY was produced by Callaway Editions, Inc.

Nicholas Callaway, Editorial Director and Publisher

Antoinette White and Alexandra Arrowsmith, Editors

Jennifer Wagner, Designer

True Sims, Production Director

Paula Litzky, Associate Publisher

Monica Moran, Publicity Director

Chris Steighner, Editorial Assistant

Ivan Wong, Jr., Production Associate

Christy Bush, Photographer

The principal fonts used for this book are *Proforma* designed by Petr van Blokland,
August designed by David James and *Scala Sans* designed by Martin Majoor. Other fonts include:
Adolescence, Albroni, Beyond Beauty, Big Cheese, Dogma Outline, Dot Matrix Grid, Elephant,
Garage Gothic, Granite, Hip Hop, Missionary, Mot Femina, Outwest, Shimano, Sister, Stereo and Whirligig.

This book was printed and bound in China by Palace Press International,
under the supervision of Raoul Goff, Erik Ko and Ruby Sia.